Aiming for Progress in Writing and Grammar

Book 4
Second Edition

William Collins' dream of knowledge for all began with the publication of his first book in 1819. A self-educated mill worker, he not only enriched millions of lives, but also founded a flourishing publishing house. Today, staying true to this spirit, Collins books are packed with inspiration, innovation and practical expertise. They place you at the centre of a world of possibility and give you exactly what you need to explore it.

Collins. Freedom to teach.

Published by Collins
An imprint of HarperCollins*Publishers*
77–85 Fulham Palace Road
Hammersmith
London
W6 8JB

Browse the complete Collins catalogue at
www.collins.co.uk

10 9 8 7 6 5 4 3 2 1
ISBN 978-0-00-754748-7

Caroline Bentley-Davies, Gareth Calway, Robert Francis, Mike Gould, Ian Kirby, Christopher Martin and Keith West assert their moral rights to be identified as the authors of this work.

British Library Cataloguing in Publication Data
A Catalogue record for this publication is available from the British Library.

Commissioned by Catherine Martin
Project managed by Sonya Newland
Edited in-house by Alicia Higgins
Copy edited by Alice Harman
Proofread by Kelly Davis
Designed by Joerg Hartmannsgruber
Typeset by 320 Media
Cover design by Angela English
Printed and bound by L.E.G.O S.p.A. Italy

With thanks to Jackie Newman and Kim Williams.

Packaged for HarperCollins by
White-Thomson Publishing Ltd.
www.wtpub.co.uk
+44 (0) 843 208 7460

Acknowledgements

The publishers gratefully acknowledge the permissions granted to reproduce copyright material in this book. While every effort has been made to trace and contact copyright holders, where this has not been possible the publishers will be pleased to make the necessary arrangements at the first opportunity.

Extracts from *Lady of the Lake* by Raymond Chandler, published by Penguin. Reprinted with permission (p 6); extracts from *Solo* by Bill Taylor and John Goodwin, published by Hodder Arnold, Hodder & Stoughton. Reprinted with permission (pp 8–9); from Emma Calway's blog emmacalway.over-blog.com/article-handbags-at-dawn-118976836.html. Reprinted with kind permission of the author (p 17); extract from 'Misadventures in South West China' in *Lonely Planet Unpacked - Travel Disaster Stories* by Jennifer Brewer, reproduced with permission from Lonely Planet Unpacked/Jennifer Brewer © 1999 Lonely Planet (pp 24–25); from 'This is our chance. This is our moment' by Barack Obama, *Daily Mail*, 6/11/2008. Reprinted with kind permission of Solo Syndication (pp 26–27); from 'Starting school at 11am is just pandering to teenagers' by Gill Hornby. *The Daily Telegraph* 9 March 2009. Copyright © Telegraph Media Group 2009. Reprinted with permission (pp 28–29); 'Underpants shredded in fight with Kangaroo' Kathy Marks, *The Independent*, 10th March 2009, *The*

Independent. Reprinted with permission (p 30); extract from *The Skeleton Key*, Anthony Horowitz, Walker Books. Copyright © 2002 Stormbreaker Productions Ltd. Reproduced by permission of Walker Books Ltd, London SE11 5HJ www.walker.co.uk and Philomel Books, a division of Penguin Group (USA) LLC (p 31); extracts from *Stone Cold* (play version adapted from Robert Swindells's novel) Joe Standerline, Nelson Thornes. Reprinted with permission (pp 38–39); from 'Homeless crisis as 400 youths a day face life on the streets of Britain' *The Mirror*, 4 December 2011. Reprinted with permission of Mirrorpix (p 42); from 'Bob the cat rescued me from drugs': how sick stray inspired addict to sell one million books' by Polly Hudson, *The Mirror*, 1 July 2013. Reprinted with permission of Mirrorpix (p 43); extract from *Z for Zachariah* by Robert O'Brien, published by Puffin Copyright © Robert O'Brien 1974, Reprinted with permission of Penguin Books UK and A. M. Heath Ltd (p 46); screenshot of home webpage for change4life. Reprinted with permission (p 47); 'I'm selfie harming', *The Sun*, 12 September, 2013. © News Syndication 2013. Reprinted with permission (p 48); from 'The last laugh' by Kamila Shamsie, *The Guardian* 8th October 2013. © Guardian News & Media Ltd 2013. Used with permission (p 49); Dickens Monologue, adapted from *Monologues with Duologue Activities*, First and Best in Education. Reprinted with permission (p 54); from 'Listening to bees buzz can help spot disease' by Richard Gray, *The Daily Telegraph* 24 March 2013. © Telegraph Media Group 2013. Reprinted with permission (pp 58–59); extracts from *The Woman in Black*, Susan Hill, Vintage Classics, Random House 1984. Reprinted with permission of Sheil Land Associates Ltd (pp 67, 68, 73); extract from *In London During the Great War*, Michael MacDonagh, Eyre and Spottiswoode, 1946 (p 70); *Death of a Hero* by Richard Aldington, copyright © 1929 renewed © 1957 by Richard Aldington. Used by permission of Penguin a division of Penguin Group (USA) LLC (p 71); Extract from *Animal Farm*, George Orwell, Penguin. Copyright © George Orwell, 1946 renewed 1974 by Sonia Orwell. by permission of Bill Hamilton as the Literary Executor of the Estate of the Late Sonia Brownell and Houghton Mifflin Harcourt Publishing Company, and Penguin Books UK, all rights reserved (p 75); Extract from *The World and Other Places*, Jeanette Winterson, Vintage, Random House (p 84); Extract from *The Cloning of Joanna May*, Fay Weldon, Flamingo, reprinted with permission of HarperCollins Publishers © 1989 Fay Weldon (p 84); extract from *The Boy Who Kicked Pigs* by Tom Baker, published by Faber and Faber, reprinted with permission of Faber and Faber Limited and Sheil Land Associates Ltd (p 86); Extract 'Tokyo Pastoral' Angela Carter, from *Shaking a Leg*, Vintage, Random House. Copyright © Angela Carter 1997. Reproduced by permission of the Estate of Angela Carter c/o Rogers, Coleridge & White Ltd, 20 Powis Mews, London W11 1JN (p 86); Extract from *Casino Royale*, Ian Fleming, Penguin. Reprinted by permission of Curtis Brown Group Limited for Ian Fleming Publications Ltd (p 87).

Cover image and p 1 © Mikhail Hoboton Popov/Shutterstock

(t = top, b = bottom)

p 5 SueC/Shutterstock, p 6 Bettmann/Corbis, p 8 Accord/Shutterstock, p 10 Universal History Archive/Getty Images, p 11 The Protected Art Archive/Alamy, p 12 Arjan van Duijvenboden/Shutterstock, p13 Classical Comics, p 14 Nejron Photo/Shutterstock, p 16 Tatu images/Shutterstock, p 19 Yuriy Seleznev/Shutterstock, p 20 Monkey Business Images/Shutterstock, p 21 anyaivanova/Shutterstock, p 23t Paul Matthew photography/Shutterstock, p 23b wavebreakmedia/Shutterstock, p 24 Robert Harding World Imagery/Alamy, p 25 Scott Warren/Alamy, p 26 Ralf-Finn Hestoft/Corbis, p 27 spirit of america/Shutterstock, p 28 AJP/Shutterstock, p 29 BarracudaDesigns/Shutterstock, p 30 Eduard Kyslynskyy/Shutterstock, p 31 Jim Agronick/Shutterstock, p 32 defpicture/Shutterstock, p 33 Alexander Cherednichenko/Shutterstock, p 34 Jenny Matthews/In Pictures/Corbis, p 35 Eric Isselee/Shutterstock, p 37 Maridav/Shutterstock, p 38 Julia Pivovarova/Shutterstock, p 39 Rtimages/Shutterstock, p 40 Monkey Business Images/Shutterstock, p 41 Sean de Burca/Shutterstock, p 42 forestpath/Shutterstock, p 43 Geoffrey Jones/Shutterstock, p 44 Allstar Picture Library/Alamy, p 45 Adrian Sherratt/Alamy, p 46 rangizzz/Shutterstock, p 48 Maridav/Shutterstock, p 49 AFP/Getty Images, p 51 oumjeab/Shutterstock, p 52 Beror/Shutterstock, p 53 Jacques PALUT/Shutterstock, p 54 Nicku/Shutterstock, p 55 kenny1/Shutterstock, p 56 Bob Thomas Sports Photography/Getty Images, p 57 lev radin/Shutterstock, p 58 Cuson/Shutterstock, p 59 Steve Oehlenschlager/Shutterstock, p 60 John Kershner/Shutterstock, p 61 Subbotina Anna/Shutterstock, p63 Ed Samuel/Shutterstock, p 64 Dave Wetzel/Shutterstock, p 66 Annette Shaff/Shutterstock, p 67 Moviestore collection Ltd/Alamy, p 68l Andrew Roland/Shutterstock, p 68r AF archive/Alamy, p 69 Zacarias Pereira da Mata/Shutterstock, p 70 Ed Samuel/Shutterstock, p 72 REX/Moviestore Collection, p 73 Aleksey Stemmer/Shutterstock, p 74 Lebrecht Music and Arts Photo Library/Alamy, p 76 Moviestore collection Ltd/Alamy, p 77 Boris Stroujko/Shutterstock, p 79 Intrepix/Shutterstock, p 80 Mopic/Shutterstock, p 81 Mary Evans/Iberfoto, p 82 Intrepix/Shutterstock, p 83 Ryan Morgan/Shutterstock, p 84 Pablo Hidalgo/Shutterstock, p 85 Monkey Business Images/Shutterstock, p 86 Chanclos/Shutterstock, p 87 AF archive/Alamy, p 89 and p 92 Hoang Tran/Shutterstock, p 90 Ieva Geneviciene/Shutterstock, p 94 Pete Saloutos/Shutterstock.

Contents

1

Chapter 1

Write imaginative, interesting and thoughtful texts

What's it all about?

It is very important to write in an imaginative and thoughtful way, choosing the right form and style and/or finding your own voice. This will make your writing apt and interesting, and give it personality.

This chapter will show you how to

- write with a clear emphasis on narration rather than plot

- write in character sustaining a role or voice

- choose an effective narrative style

- write using a range of stylistic devices to create effects

- choose effective vocabulary for your purpose

- write reflectively and analytically to explore issues or ideas.

Write with a clear emphasis on narration rather than plot

Learning objective
- add some liveliness and character to your writing.

'It's the way he tells them!' The best stories are enjoyable because of their *narration* (the way they are told) as much as their **plot**.

Glossary

plot: what happens in a story

Getting you thinking

Read this extract from a detective novel. The first person ('I') narrator is the private detective Phillip Marlowe.

> 'You want to see me?' he barked.
>
> He was about six feet two and not much of it soft. His eyes were stone grey with flecks of cold light in them. He filled a large size in smooth grey flannel with a narrow chalk stripe, and filled it elegantly. His manner said he was very tough to get along with.
>
> I stood up. 'If you're Mr Derace Kingsley.'
>
> 'Who the hell did you think I was?'
>
> *The Lady in the Lake* by Raymond Chandler

1 What actually *happens* in this extract? Think about how the extract would appear if Chandler was focusing only on the plot.

For instance, to show the two men's introduction he might have written:

> 'You want to see me?' Mr Kingsley said.
>
> 'Yes,' I answered.

2 What is the difference between the extract and the simplified version above?

The dialogue that follows the extract is like a shoot-out, with the two men aggressively confronting each other:

> 'I don't like your manner,' Kingsley said in a voice you could have cracked a brazil nut on.
>
> 'That's all right,' I said. 'I'm not selling it.'

3 Chandler uses the **metaphor** 'a voice you could have cracked a brazil nut on'.

    a) Look back at the first extract and find another metaphor that describes Mr Kingsley.

    b) What does this imagery tell you about the character?

Glossary

metaphor: a comparison between two things that does not use 'as' or 'like'

How does it work?

The narration conveys much more than just the plot. It gives the novel its energy, wit and atmosphere, portraying a streetwise world where men talk – and act – tough. Descriptive verbs such as 'barked' and the tone of Kingsley's reply ('Who the hell did you think I was?') help create the dark, edgy tone common in the *noir* genre of fiction.

Now you try it

4 Re-read the paragraph describing Mr Kingsley in the first extract. What patterns can you see here? Think about the type of sentences, how they are structured and phrased, and what repetitions they include.

In pairs, read the extract on the right, from the same novel.

5 Discuss the extract with your partner.

    a) What is the plot of the extract?

    b) What overall *feeling* do you get from this passage? How is this feeling achieved? Think about metaphors, tone and sentence patterns.

> I lit a cigarette and dragged a smoking stand beside the chair. The minutes went by on tiptoe, with their fingers to their lips [...]
>
> Half an hour and three or four cigarettes later a door opened behind Miss Fromsett's desk and two men came out backwards, laughing. A third man held the door for them and helped them laugh. They all shook hands heartily and the two men went across the office and out. The third man dropped the grin off his face and looked as if he had never grinned in his life. He was a tall bird in a grey suit and he didn't want any nonsense.
>
> 'Any calls?' he asked in a sharp bossy voice.

Apply your skills

6 Complete and continue the following narration describing the secretary, Miss Fromsett, in a *noir* style.

> She wore a steel-grey business suit and...
>
> She wore...
>
> Her dark hair was...
>
> The edges of the folded handkerchief in the breast pocket looked sharp enough to...

Include details of her posture, gestures and facial features. Remember – your purpose is to narrate a personality that fits the tough, wise-cracking world of the *noir* novel.

Check your progress

Some progress
I can continue the narration in an appropriate style.

Good progress
I can narrate with energy and imagination.

Excellent progress
I can sustain a convincing and imaginative narrative in the *noir* style.

Write in character sustaining a role or voice

Learning objective
- write as someone else, using appropriate language and tone.

Writing in character means that you 'become' another person, taking on their language and way of speaking just as you would put on a costume.

Getting you thinking

Look at these two **monologues**. *Solo* by Bill Taylor and John Goodwin.

Thomo

> Watchit...! They call me Thomo. Me – I'm always in trouble. Can't resist a fight. I don't know why but I just see red. If somebody picks on me, I have to fight back, don't I? Why should they pick on me? Why should they pick on me just 'cause I'm small?

Head teacher

> I don't know what's happened. I've been a teacher for eighteen years now and there was a time when I used to enjoy my job. I used to feel I understood the children I taught. I could relax, have a joke, they'd tell me about themselves. But now it's different...
>
> Take Craig Thomson for instance. He's waiting outside my office now for fighting. He's the tenth boy I've seen this week about causing trouble in school. I shall have to suspend him – I have no choice, even though I know he's not a bad lad at heart.

Glossary

monologues: long speeches delivered by one person

1. In pairs, act out these extracts. Try to capture the 'voice' of each character.

2. What are the differences between the two extracts? Look at the the vocabulary each character uses, the sentence type and length and the punctuation.

How does it work?

The head teacher's speech is written in a different style from Thomo's. For example, Thomo speaks mostly in short, punchy sentences. He uses informal language and chippy **rhetorical questions**. The head teacher speaks in longer, full sentences. His style is more formal and thoughtful.

Glossary

rhetorical questions: questions that are really statements – they do not expect an answer

Re-read the head teacher's monologue.

3 How do you think he feels about what goes on in the school? Write a continuation of the head teacher's speech, in which he makes it clear why he has to suspend Thomo. Try to write in the same 'voice' as the extract. You could begin:

> I shall have to play the part of the strict head teacher and suspend him, because otherwise...

4 Now write another continuation of the head teacher's monologue. This time, make him sound less certain about what to do. Use questions to express his uncertainty:

> But why should I? Wouldn't it be a change to say, Thomo, look, I understand – I was picked on when I was a kid, too...

Apply your skills

Look at this monologue. Lana is a teenager who has been picked up by the police for joy-riding.

> I hate it when they get you on your own. I just stare back at them. Don't say much. What do they want to know? Why I did it? Why I got in that car with Thomo and the others on Friday night? Nah – they're not interested even when I do tell 'em. Not in the real reasons – the boredom, the fact I can't go home 'cos they threw me out, that Thomo's my only real mate. There's this one social worker who's there sometimes. She understands, listens. But the rest are a waste of space.

5 Write a dialogue between Lana and the social worker, focusing on Lana's problems. Use language, sentence structure and punctuation to create a voice and show their different characters and role.

For example, the social worker might use long full sentences, while Lana uses broken sentences, exclamations and questions. Think about typical things that each character might say.

You could begin: 'Take a seat, Lana.'

Top tip

It may help to improvise your speeches in role first.

Check your progress

Some progress 〉〉
I can create a particular voice.

Good progress 〉〉〉
I can assume and mostly sustain a convincing voice and viewpoint for each character.

Excellent progress 〉〉〉〉
I can adopt and completely sustain a distinctive individual voice and viewpoint in my dialogue.

Choose an effective narrative style

Choosing an effective style means varying your writing to create thoughtful and interesting texts. For example, you could choose between a formal or conversational style.

Getting you thinking

The *form* of a novel is the shape and organisation of the story. The *style* is how it is told – the way in which it 'speaks' to the reader.

Look at this opening from a novel by Charles Dickens. The narrator is a Victorian gentleman-author. The form is the 'growing-up' novel known as a *bildungsroman*.

> Whether I shall turn out to be the hero of my own life, or whether that station will be held by anybody else, these pages must show. To begin my life with the beginning of my life, I record that I was born (as I have been informed and believe) on a Friday, at twelve o'clock at night. It was remarked that the clock began to strike and I began to cry simultaneously.
>
> *David Copperfield* by Charles Dickens

 What style does the narrator use to tell his story? How old do you think he is?

How does it work?

The writing style supports the central idea of life as a journey with definite stages.

Now you try it

Not all *bildungsromans* are written in the same style. This extract is from a late 19th-century novel about a 12-year-old boy growing up in the American South. The style is very different from *David Copperfield*, but it is still a *bildungsroman*, and the narrator is still telling his own story.

> You don't know about me, without you have read a book by the name of *The Adventures of Tom Sawyer,* but that ain't no matter. That book was made by Mr Mark Twain, and he told the truth, mainly. There was things he stretched, but mainly he told the truth. That is nothing. I never seen anybody but lied, one time or another...
>
> *The Adventures of Huckleberry Finn* by Mark Twain

2 In groups of four, answer the following questions, giving examples.

a) How does the author get you interested in his narrator?

b) Does this sound like the voice of a real 12-year-old?

c) What age or type of readers is the book aimed at?

d) Does the author make fun of the formal way in which adults write?

e) Do you like the narrator? Is he funny or surprising?

f) How is the narrator's language here different from *David Copperfield*?

g) Why do you think Twain gave his narrator this style?

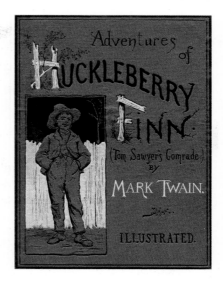

Apply your skills

Your school magazine has asked you to write about 'An Event That Changed My Life'.

3 First, make a plan. Choose a form that suits your purpose. It could be

- an imaginary story based on real events
- a poem.

4 Now write your *opening*, first choosing an appropriate style and a convincing narrative voice.

- You could describe the event from the child's point of view at the time. If so, you might want to use a chatty, **colloquial** style and a child's voice.

- Or you could write it as an older child reflecting on younger experience. In this case, you would need to use a more mature and thoughtful narrative style. Where the character of the child appears in your story or poem, they should speak in a believable child's voice.

If you choose to write a poem, you could divide it into two stanzas and include both narrators. Try to construct a convincing voice for each of them:

- stanza 1 – the point of view of the child at the time
- stanza 2 – the adult looking back.

Glossary

colloquial: informal, casual or everyday

Check your progress

Some progress

I can create a narrative style in my writing.

Good progress

I can choose appropriate language to suit a narrative style.

Excellent progress

I can mostly sustain a narrative style through the apt use of vocabulary and other language features.

Write using a range of stylistic devices to create effects

Learning objective

- make your writing more vivid using sound, rhythm, setting and imagery.

You can make your writing vivid by thinking about the power that *sound*, *rhythm* and *imagery* can bring to words.

Getting you thinking

Poetry is packed with word power, so writing poetry is a good training for all effective writing. Look at this poem:

> **Morte d'Arthur**
>
> Dry clash'd his harness in the icy caves
> And barren chasms, and all to left and right
> The bare black cliff clang'd round him, as he based
> His feet on juts of slippery crag that rang
> Sharp-smitten with the dint of armed heels –
> And on a sudden, lo! the level lake,
> And the long glories of the winter moon.
>
> Alfred, Lord Tennyson

 1 What do you notice about the sound, rhythm and imagery in the description of an armoured knight in winter? Pick out words, phrases or effects you particularly like.

How does it work?

The poem uses various stylistic devices to intensify the effect of its words.

Device	Purpose	Example
Onomatopoeia	To match the sound of the language to the content by using words that sound like the things they describe	The hard consonant sounds (j, t, g, d and especially c) in lines 3–5 sound like armour clanging ('clang'd') on rock
Dash	To separate parts of a sentence, but also to bring them together in contrast	Marks the change in the poem at the end of line 5, from noise and danger to peaceful beauty
Imagery	To create vivid pictures in the reader's mind	The 'bare black cliff' (line 3) paints a picture of a rough and desolate place
Lines	To focus on the essentials of the poem by forcing the poet to limit the number of words used in each line	used as the basic form/structure of the poem

Look at the comic strip of *Romeo and Juliet* below. A plain description of the action might be:

> The Montagues and the Capulets fight each other in the market place.

2 Look at the pig and the chicken in the comic strip.

   a) How do you think they feel?

   b) What sounds are used to convey their feelings? Are these sounds effective?

3 Write a description of the scene, using sound and rhythm to increase its effectiveness.

   a) Include echoes of the THWAK, AAAWK and SQUEE sounds (or KTANGG from a sword clash in a previous panel) by finding some real words that contain parts of these sounds.

   b) Is 'k' the dominant sound here, or is it 'sh' or 'th'?

   c) Are any of the weapon sounds in the panels real words already?

4 Include an *image* (metaphor or **simile**) that helps your reader picture the sword hitting the man's shoulder in the second panel.

5 Add other apt images and sounds to build up the *overall mood* of the skirmish. Use repetition and rhythm to emphasise this battle mood.

Apply your skills

6 Imagine you are any one of the characters in the comic strip. Write five lines of verse using your sounds and images that convey the battle scene and your feelings.

Glossary

simile: a comparison of one thing with another, using 'as' or 'like'

Check your progress

Some progress

I can use some imagery and sound effects in my verse.

Good progress

I can use some different stylistic devices to convey a scene effectively.

Excellent progress

I can use a range of stylistic devices for impact and effect.

Choose effective vocabulary for your purpose

Learning objective

- write imaginatively in a form and language that suits your purpose.

Writing imaginatively means choosing an apt form for your material, as well as selecting suitable and striking words and phrases to keep readers interested.

Getting you thinking

In these opening verses of '**Childe** Roland to the Dark Tower Came', a knight meets a 'hoary cripple' (an ancient, twisted man) who gives him directions.

> ### Childe Roland to the Dark Tower Came
>
> My first thought was, he lied in every word,
> That hoary cripple, with malicious eye
> **Askance** to watch the working of his lie
> On mine, and mouth scarce able to afford
> **Suppression** of the glee, that pursed and scored
> Its edge, at one more victim gained thereby.
> What else should he be set for, and his **staff**?
> What, save to waylay with his lies, ensnare
> All travellers that might find him posted there,
> And ask the road? I guessed what skull-like laugh
> Would break, what crutch '**gin** write my **epitaph**
> For pastime in the dusty thoroughfare,
> If at this **counsel** I should turn aside
> Into that **ominous tract** which, all agree,
> Hides the Dark Tower.
>
> Robert Browning

Glossary

Childe: an old word for knight

Askance: sideways, out of the corner (of his eye)

Suppression: the holding back

staff: tall stick or crutch

'gin: begin

epitaph: the words on a gravestone

counsel: advice about which way to go

ominous tract: scary track (with bad omens)

1 In pairs, look at the vocabulary Browning uses.

a) What kind of world is he trying to conjure up? Does he succeed?

b) Read the poem again, using the everyday **synonyms** 'old', 'trap' and 'sideways' in place of 'hoary', 'ensnare' and 'askance'. What effect does this have?

c) Substitute ordinary synonyms for: 'suppression', 'glee', 'pursed', 'scored', 'thereby', 'counsel', 'ominous'. How does this change the tone of the writing?

Glossary

synonym: a word that means almost exactly the same as another word

2 What signs can you find that the form Browning uses here is either a **quest** or a **suspense narrative**?

How does it work?

Browning's choice of vocabulary creates a sinister and otherworldly atmosphere. The everyday synonyms you chose probably made the poem feel much less atmospheric.

Now you try it

Look at this verse from later on in the poem. The rhyme words have been removed and listed in the table below.

A sudden little river crossed my _____

As unexpected as a serpent _____

No sluggish tide **congenial** to the _____

This, as it frothed by, might have been a _____

For the **fiend**'s glowing hoof – to see the _____

Of its black **eddy bespate** with flakes and _____

comes	path	bath	**wrath**	**spumes**	glooms

3 Checking with the rhyme pattern of the first verse, insert these rhyme words so that they make sense.

4 In pairs, decide what words in this stanza are suitably 'strange' to describe this quest landscape. Which words, by contrast, are everyday terms?

Apply your skills

5 Choose your own form and vocabulary to describe a key moment in a quest across a wasteland.

Checklist for success

- ✔ Include names of places or characters, or high-flown expressions from myth and legend or tales of swords and sorcery.
- ✔ Use a thesaurus/dictionary to find unusual and atmospheric synonyms for some of your descriptive nouns and verbs.
- ✔ Decide how many lines will go in each of your stanzas and roughly how long each line will be. Think about whether the lines will be of uniform length, and what kind of rhyme pattern (if any) you will use.

Glossary

quest narrative: a story about an adventurous journey

suspense narrative: a story that is tense and exciting because something important will happen

congenial to: suited to

fiend: the devil

eddy: counter-current, swirl

bespate: flooded

wrath: anger

spumes: froth, foam

Top tip

Choose suitable otherworldly words and phrases, and use rhyme to create a spell-like atmosphere.

Check your progress

Some progress

I can describe a key moment in a quest.

Good progress

I can use quest-narrative form and vocabulary accurately.

Excellent progress

I can use quest-narrative form and vocabulary accurately and creatively.

Write reflectively and analytically to explore issues or ideas

Learning objectives

- Express opinions and analyse issues in your writing.

Writing reflectively and analytically means that you are able to explain more complicated subjects to your reader using advanced writing skills.

Getting you thinking

Read this post on a social media site, and the apology that followed after many complaints were made about it.

> The British are much too sentimental about animals. Animals are unhygienic, dangerous and violent. Take them all back to the wild, I say, and let them fend for themselves.

> [after several complaints]
>
> It would appear that I have once again offended people on here. Offence is never my intention. I behave on here like it is a social club: shoot the breeze, say the wrong things, get in a heated debate and then forget about it. Please, seriously, if that is not for you, delete me. I really don't want to offend anyone.

1. Look at the original post.
   a) What do you think of the writer's analysis of the British and their attitude towards animals?
   b) What *type of sentences* does he use?
   c) Do the writer's reflections convince you? Does he present them as opinions or facts?

2. Now look at the apology.
   a) What point does the writer make about the social media site?
   b) Try reading it without the softening phrase 'It would appear that', the **adverbial** 'really' and polite modifiers such as 'please' and 'seriously', which qualify and soften the imperative 'delete me'. How different is the tone of the writing? In what way?

Glossary

adverbial: word or phrase used like an adverb to modify a verb or clause

How does it work?

To express a strong viewpoint you can use *statement sentences*, giving opinion as fact. Here, the writer also gives a command ('Take them all back to the wild') with a personal stamp ('I say'). He uses *exaggeration* and *generalisation* as another way to hammer home his opinion.

Modals can help express a point in a less forceful, more polite way. Subjunctives can also soften the impact of a statement, making it appear as more of an opinion than a solid fact.

Glossary

Modals: forms or moods of a verb that express levels of certainty/possibility (might/ should/would and so on); modals modify a verb in the same way as an adverb does

Now you try it

Read this blog post.

Last night's *Apprentice* heralded a win for the women's team – it was an absolute joy not to see the female front bickering, slagging each other off and nit-picking at each other through the lashings of lip gloss, hair spray and eyeliner that seems to take precedent over manners [...].

Don't get me wrong, the men don't come out smelling of roses [...] but the female bickering seems to always attract more interest. The camera occasionally catches Karren Brady looking despairingly at the sisterhood, shaming everything she has fought for long and hard as the only female in a boardroom full of testosterone.

But on the plus side we enter the final rounds with three women and two men ... and with a serious contender in the form of Louisa ... It looks like it's set to be a Neil v Louisa final with both having a bit more clout about them than Myles – dull as dishwater – and Leah – if I pout this much my mouth might actually fall off. If Louisa can concentrate on her game plan more than her reflection in the mirror for a second she might have a real chance at beating the blokes.

'Handbags at Dawn' by Emma Calway

3 What is the writer's viewpoint?

4 What exaggerations and generalisations does she use to support her analysis? Note down any language that softens or hardens the expression of her viewpoint.

5 Imagine that fans of Myles and Leah wrote to Calway to complain about her blog. Rewrite Calway's viewpoint using softening language devices such as modals and adverbials. For example: 'While I have no wish to..., nevertheless...'

Apply your skills

6 Write your own blog post of roughly 200 words in which you express a strong opinion about an issue. Afterwards, rewrite your post using softer language.

Check your progress

Some progress

I can state a viewpoint in my writing.

Good progress

I can present a viewpoint in an appropriate way.

Excellent progress

I can express a viewpoint in a range of appropriate ways that win over the reader.

Check your progress

Some progress

- [ ] I can write imaginatively and thoughtfully and interest the reader.
- [ ] I can plan, develop and shape my writing.
- [ ] I can choose the right word or sentence to create an effect.
- [ ] I can write vividly, powerfully, memorably.
- [ ] I can develop a convincing viewpoint or role.
- [ ] I can use language to explain and explore ideas.

Good progress

- [ ] I can write with a clear emphasis on narration rather than only plot.
- [ ] I can write in character sustaining a role, voice or point of view.
- [ ] I can write in a form and style that achieves the right effect.
- [ ] I can write using a range of stylistic devices to create effects.
- [ ] I can make a good attempt to be creative with appropriate form and language.
- [ ] I can write reflectively to explore, explain and analyse issues.

Excellent progress

- [ ] I can narrate stories with fluency and imagination.
- [ ] I can usually sustain well-judged, distinctive individual viewpoints.
- [ ] I can usually sustain a consistent and appropriate form, formality and style.
- [ ] I can creatively apply the sound and picture power of language.
- [ ] I can usually vary form, style and effect where appropriate.
- [ ] I can write clear and balanced explanations.

2

Chapter 2
Produce texts that are appropriate to task, reader and purpose

What's it all about?

It is important for you to understand that your writing style must fit the needs of a specific audience.

This chapter will show you how to

- write creatively for specific effects
- use a range of techniques to match your genre and purpose
- write persuasively for a particular audience
- adapt what you have read for different purposes
- adapt the formality of your writing to match the purpose and task.

Write creatively for specific effects

Learning objective

- choose the right form and language for a range of purposes.

Being creative means using language to create interesting or powerful effects. But the effects must fit the intended purpose of the writing. A comic account of an event will require different language to a heartfelt reflection.

Ask yourself: what effect or tone do I want to create? What **conventions** or language techniques will help me achieve this purpose?

Glossary

conventions: well-known ideas or patterns used in texts – for example, love poems often deal with meetings, rejections and so on

Getting you thinking

Read this short poem.

> **Brief Relationship**
>
> First date – me late,
> She left, didn't wait.
> I texted, she replied,
> 'Get lost!' – no surprise.
> Next day, she's with Trevor,
> So ends, 'R & J forever'.
>
> Mike Gould

1 Do you think the purpose of this short poem is to:

a) give an in-depth exploration of a serious love affair?

b) look back with humour at 'first love'?

c) tell us all about a fascinating person?

How does it work?

The effect of the poem is humour tinged with **pathos**. The poet creates this effect in a number of ways.

The informal and **staccato** style suggests matter-of-fact bluntness, phone texting or a scribbled note in class.

The rhymed pairs of lines suggest rap or performance poetry.

Glossary

pathos: sadness or pity in the reader's response

staccato: jerky, short sounds

The lack of information about the narrator and other 'characters' adds to the idea of this being an everyday, fleeting romance. Yet the final line is **ironic**, as it makes us think of the famous Shakespearean lovers – who were probably of a similar age to the narrator and the girl in the poem.

> **Now you try it**

Here is another love poem.

Meeting at Night

The grey sea and the long black land;
And the yellow half-moon large and low;
And the startled little waves that leap
In fiery ringlets from their sleep,
As I gain the cove with pushing prow,
And quench its speed in the slushy sand.
Then a mile of warm sea-scented beach;
Three fields to cross till a farm appears;
A tap at the pane, the quick sharp scratch
And a blue spurt of a lighted match,
And a voice less loud, thro' its joys and fears,
Than the two hearts beating each to each!

Robert Browning

2 In pairs, answer these questions:

a) What emotions does the poem express – excitement, nervousness, intimacy?

b) How does the poet convey these feelings? Think about the impact of

- adjectives
- metaphors
- rhymes
- the setting
- the story.

In both poems, the writers' choices about language and form help to create a particular effect.

3 In pairs, discuss how Browning's poem is more specific in some descriptions, and less specific in others, than 'Brief Relationship'. Think about

a) the use of names and details about people: who is the narrator of the second poem meeting?

b) the effect this choice or lack of detail has on the reader. Does it fit the story being told or the situation it describes?

c) the *soundscape* of the poem: find examples of specific sound 'events' (such as rhymes and half-rhymes, repeated sounds or shifts in rhythm) that reflect the content and focus the reader's attention.

4 Copy and complete this grid for 'Meeting at Night'.

Feature or convention	'Meeting at Night'
Story and theme of poem	
Narrative voice	
Setting/s	
Vocabulary (think about **noun phrases** such as 'fiery ringlets')	
Imagery (if any)	**Transferred epithets** ('startled little waves')
Sound and rhythm	Soundscape created by phrases such as...
Form and structure	

Glossary

noun phrase: a sequence of words that do the work of a noun, but extend it

transferred epithet: an adjective that describes the wrong noun; for instance, in a 'sleepless' night it is a person rather than the night itself who is sleepless

5 Now, add or remove words in this first verse of a poem and alter the structure as you see fit. Try to change its tone and rhythm through the choices you make (can you create a transferred epithet?)

You left your _____ untouched and left the place,

No tears or anger, simply sadness in your _____

I stirred the _____ clouds of coffee, pushed back my chair

Headed for the exit and the _____

6 Imagine you have been asked to contribute a poem to a collection of love poetry. The editors want a mix of poems that have old or modern settings, but they must be no longer than 20 lines each.

Plan and write a poem called 'The Betrayal'.

Think about

- whether your setting is going to be historical or modern

- who is narrating or speaking in the poem

- what basic story your poem will tell (for example, someone betraying another person, or being betrayed)

- what tone you wish to achieve (light-hearted and everyday? Serious and dramatic? Sad and reflective?)

- what *form* – for instance, the style of verse and the stanza lengths – will suit it

- what *language* will work best (powerful imagery? Short sharp verbs? Regular rhymes, or something freer?)

Build up a 'palette' of suitable words, noun phrases and lines you could use. Think about

- imagery: objects or natural events that suggest betrayal (a candle going out? a torn photo? a black crow staring at a wren's nest?)

- soundscape descriptions: weather (high wind in the trees?); places (a glass smashing on a hard floor?); people (footsteps on gravel?)

Swap your poem with a partner and compare the form and language that you have each used.

Check your progress

Use a range of techniques to match your genre and purpose

Learning objective

- use the conventions of travel writing to engage and interest the reader.

Writers of real-life experiences convey to the reader the drama and emotion of a situation, and provide vivid details that bring the experience to life.

Getting you thinking

 1 What would you expect to see in an interesting piece of travel writing? Draw up a quick list of everything you can think of.

Now read the following extract from a book of travel stories.

By now I was exhausted from two straight days of grit and fuss. I sat on the edge of my seat, impatient and grumpy, wondering if it was really necessary to go through all this just to find serenity in China. At every little town we came to I asked the poor old man sitting opposite me if we were in Yangshuo yet. At dusk a series of strange, conical, rocky green hills started popping up in the distant sunset, looking more like cartoon drawings than anything real. After almost nine hours of bus travel I began to sense that the end was in sight; all I wanted was a plate of fried noodles, [...] a shower and a bed.

We arrived in Yangshuo to a fanfare of noise and lights. This was it! My man across the aisle suddenly seemed as excited as I was, as the bus driver slammed on the brakes. I leapt up, grabbed my backpack and fell out of the bus and onto the doorstep of the Zhuyang Hotel.

'Hello, welcome, my friend – you are tired, come inside!' shouted an exuberant Peter Xuehu, the chubby, middle aged proprietor. The bus roared off, and I stumbled inside as if disembarking from a week at sea. 'So, long trip, eh?' Peter Xuehu asked in good, if thickly accented English. 'Go upstairs to dorm at end of hall, take shower, pay me later!'

I found the room, dropped my back pack, and reached for my money belt, only to feel the skinny slickness of my waist. With a sickening, heart-dropping horror, I suddenly realised that it was still tied to the overhead rack of the bus.

No! I whirled about in a sudden panic and took quick stock of the predicament. Was this possible? I ripped open my back pack, as if I had put it there and forgotten – not there. What was in it? All my money, my passport, my plane ticket onward from Hong Kong, even my little Nikon One-Touch camera. Impossible! Defying all appeals to common sense, I had stashed every dollar, yuan, travellers cheque and credit card in the belt, with nary a penny in reserve elsewhere.

'Misadventure in South West China' by Tim Nollen, in *Lonely Planet Unpacked*

2 What kinds of sentences are used in each paragraph to reflect the narrator's feelings?

How does it work?

In the text, the writer

- uses time connectives to convey the stages of the journey ('At dusk')

- describes setting and atmosphere in detail, using similes and extended noun phrases

- uses varied sentence structures and punctuation to convey the excitement of the arrival

- brings the account to life using direct speech

- uses sentences of varying length and rhetorical questions to convey the developing drama and his panic.

Now you try it

3 Plan an account of a journey, trip or holiday (real or imagined) when something goes wrong. Use the structure below.

- **Stage 1:** arrival at, or description of, the place you are staying in, including vivid details of the place and/or people.

- **Stage 2:** the problem: what happens or has happened? Your reaction to it, and what it means; the first feelings of panic or confusion building up.

- **Stage 3:** the dramatic climax: realisation of the real trouble or difficulty you are in, and what you are going to have to do.

Apply your skills

4 Now write a draft of your account, making sure to include the effective techniques Nollen uses.

Check your progress

Some progress

I can include some travel-writing conventions in my account.

Good progress

I can use a range of different conventions to create a believable account.

Excellent progress

I can carefully select from a variety of techniques to create a convincing and exciting narrative account.

Write persuasively for a particular audience

Learning objective

- use rhetorical devices to develop a persuasive point.

Over time, speech writers have developed a range of techniques to make their speeches effective. You should try to start using conventions in your own persuasive writing.

Getting you thinking

What makes an effective speech?

Read this extract from Barack Obama's speech, made on the evening he was elected President of the United States.

> If there is anyone out there who still doubts that America is a place where all things are possible, who still wonders if the dream of our founders is alive in our time, who still questions the power of our democracy, tonight is your answer.
>
> It's the answer told by lines that stretched around schools and churches in numbers this nation has never seen, by people who waited three hours and four hours, many for the first time in their lives, because they believed that this time must be different, that their voices could be that difference.
>
> It's the answer spoken by young and old, rich and poor, Democrat and Republican, black, white, Hispanic, Asian, Native American, gay, straight, disabled and not disabled, Americans who sent a message to the world that we have never been just a collection of individuals or a collection of red states and blue states.
>
> We are, and will always be, the United States of America.
>
> It's been a long time coming, but tonight, change has come to America...To all my other brothers and sisters, thank you so much for all the support that you've given me.
>
> I was never the likeliest candidate for this office. Our campaign was not hatched in the halls of Washington. It began in back yards, living rooms and front porches. It was built by working men and women who dug into what little savings they had to give $5 and $10 and $20.

It drew strength from the young people who rejected the myth of their generation's apathy, who left their homes and families for jobs that offered little pay and less sleep. It drew strength from the not-so-young people who braved the bitter cold and scorching heat to knock on the door of perfect strangers, and from the millions of Americans who volunteered, organised and proved that more than two centuries later a government of the people, by the people, and for the people has not perished from the Earth.

This is your victory.

1 In pairs, decide

a) what message the speech is putting across and why it has been written

b) what different kinds of people Barack Obama is addressing

c) what methods Obama uses to appeal to his audience.

How does it work?

Obama appeals to his audience by using a range of well-known conventions, including **rhetorical techniques**.

- He gives a confident assertion that democracy is still a strong force in America.

- He reinforces his assertion with concrete examples.

- He makes everyone feel involved in his victory by using personal or possessive pronouns.

- He uses the first person 'I' to subtly highlight his role in making these changes happen, without over-emphasising it.

- He uses repetition, lists and the power of three to emphasise and reiterate his points and make them sound persuasive.

- He mixes short and long sentences for dramatic impact.

Glossary

rhetorical techniques: language patterns or vocabulary choices designed to create a reaction in the reader or listener

Top tip

Remember the convention of the power of three. Using a list of three ideas or key points can really hammer home your message. For example, 'Free chocolate, no homework and ten-week summer holidays – these are all things that would improve school life!'

Now you try it

Read the memo below.

To members of the school council.

There is a current debate in the media about whether students' education would benefit from a later start to school. Some 'experts' suggest that the school day should start at 11am, instead of before 9am.

What are your views on this? Please read around the subject and prepare a short speech giving the views of your year group. The school's senior management will be present, along with three governors and parents of some Year 11 students.

We look forward to hearing your views.

Mrs Earlyriser (Head teacher)

Now read this article giving one journalist's viewpoint on the idea that school should start later in the morning.

Starting school at 11am is just pandering to teenagers

A little bit of unpleasantness is part of what education should be about, writes Gill Hornby.

Families with teenagers are getting on so well in Britain today. So what a bore that Dr Paul Kelley of Monkseaton High School has chosen this very moment to pop up with his Theory of the Teenager and the Lie-in to set us at each other's throats again.

Dr Kelley, a headmaster of radical views, is putting such faith in a trial by Oxford neuroscientists, with which his pupils were involved, that he is planning to reschedule his school's day so that teenagers no longer have to roll out of bed much before 11. The research indicates that they are not being lazy – absolutely not – but are biologically programmed to sleep: getting them up is injurious to their academic performance and health. He reckons his school will get more top grades if everyone takes it easy to round about lunchtime.

He's right of course. Having to get up to go to school is an unpleasantness, one of the few that are left. The rest have all been ironed out. Various electronic devices have killed off the threat of even a moment's boredom. Facebook means teenagers can socialise madly even when stuck at home. School shoes come with toys in them, medicine is delicious, even toothpaste tastes of bubblegum – because everything, at all times, must be Fun.

In that context, an alarm clock and a repetitive, yelling parent is, indeed, an anachronism. It's not an easy job, waking up teenagers, but at least it is finished by 8am. Dr Kelley's 11am start would make it difficult for a parent to have a job, or even younger children. Well, we'll just have to give them all up, I suppose.

[... Surely] one point of a school and a timetable is to produce adults who can function in society; not an entire generation that ... feels entitled to be buried in a duvet till lunchtime.

Gill Hornby in the *Telegraph* online

2 In pairs, note down the different arguments for and against a later start.

What is Gill Hornby's own viewpoint? How does she make this clear?

Apply your skills

3 Using evidence from the news article, write the speech requested in the memo from the head teacher on page 28.

Checklist for success

- ✔ Decide on the viewpoint you want to adopt in your speech.
- ✔ Think about who your audience will be. How can you best tailor your argument and your speech to appeal to them?
- ✔ What rhetorical techniques will you use?

Check your progress

Some progress
I can maintain my viewpoint and use some persuasive techniques.

Good progress
I can engage the reader and use persuasive techniques to get a response.

Excellent progress
I can sustain my viewpoint using subtle and more direct techniques to persuade the reader.

Adapt what you have read for different purposes

Learning objective
- transform information in one text into another that has a different purpose.

Good writers are able to take a text and use material from it for a different purpose. For example, a writer might read a real-life story and want to turn it into a play or short story. This involves thinking about the conventions of each form.

Getting you thinking

Read these two openings of texts about animal attacks.

Underpants shredded in fight with kangaroo

When Beat Ettlin was woken up by a dark figure crashing through his bedroom window at 2am, he assumed it was a burglar. Moments later, a 6ft kangaroo was bouncing on his bed. It was not a situation that Mr Ettlin, who lives in a leafy suburb of Canberra, the Australian national capital, ever expected to encounter. So he and his wife, Verity Beman, and their nine year old daughter Beatrix, ducked under the sheets while the kangaroo – which seemed as terrified as they were – gouged holes in the wooden bed frame with its claws, leaving a trail of blood on the walls.

The roo, which had injured itself smashing through the 9ft window of the master bedroom, jumped on top of them repeatedly. Then it was off, bounding into 10 year old Leighton's room. 'There's a roo in my room,' shouted the astonished boy, from his bed. Mr Ettlin, a 42 year old chef, originally from Switzerland, said yesterday: 'I thought "this can be really dangerous for the whole family now".'

Spurred into action, he jumped the seven stone marsupial from behind and pinned it to the floor. Then, as the kangaroo flailed and lashed out, he grabbed it in a headlock and wrestled it into the hallway, towards the front door. Using a single fumbling hand, Mr Ettlin – wearing only underpants, which were shredded from the tussle – opened the door and shoved his adversary into the night.

Kathy Marks, *The Independent*

Alex was about to swim forward when there was another movement just outside his field of vision. Whatever he had seen before had come back, swimming the other way. Puzzled, he looked up. And froze. He actually felt the air stop somewhere at the back of his throat. The last of the bubbles chased each other up to the surface. Alex just hung there, fighting for control. He wanted to scream. But underwater, it isn't possible to scream.

He was looking at a great white shark, at least three metres long, circling slowly above him. The sight was so unreal, so utterly shocking, that at first Alex quite literally didn't believe his eyes.

It had to be an illusion, some sort of trick. The very fact that it was so close to him seemed impossible. He stared at the white underbelly, the two sets of fins, the down-turned crescent mouth with its jagged, razor-sharp teeth. And there were the deadly, round eyes, as black and as evil as anything on the planet. Had they seen him yet?

Skeleton Key by Anthony Horowitz

1 Answer the following questions.

a) What type of text is each extract? How do you know?

b) Are there any similarities between the texts? If so, what are they?

c) What differences are there in the style and language of the texts?

d) In what ways are the conventions of news reporting and story-telling followed? (For example, does the report start with the key facts?)

How does it work?

Look again at the description of the kangaroo attack. It has all the ingredients of an exciting short story but it also has some conventions that make it clear that it's from a newspaper:

- a snappy and humorous headline to intrigue the reader at a glance
- key information in the first paragraph – the who, what, where and when
- a mix of tenses – the past tense to describe what happened and the present tense when reporting speech
- an eyewitness quotation from the main person involved.

Now you try it

2 Imagine you are rewriting the newspaper article as a short story. Think about the conventions of stories, and consider which of Horowitz's techniques you could use.

    a) How would you start? Would you include in the story's opening *all* the information given in the report's first paragraph? Why? Why not?

    b) What additional information might you need to make up? What would you leave out?

    c) Which parts of the story would you slow down or speed up to engage the reader? Which part of the story is the most exciting? How would you create and maintain tension?

    d) Whose viewpoint would you tell the story from?

3 Rewrite the kangaroo attack as a short story, using some of the ideas you came up with in the previous activity.

Apply your skills

Imagine you are a journalist who has been sent into the Australian outback following reports that a giant crocodile – the largest ever seen – has been discovered in the living-room of a family's house. Here are the notes you have taken:

> Mrs Dundee, widow, 33, with two small children runs small farm on her own, 20 miles south of Darwin.
>
> Discovered croc at 7am in morning. Was about to feed her two dogs, Arnie and Rocky.
>
> Got rifle. Fired warning shots but croc wouldn't leave. Dogs nowhere to be seen at first.
>
> Neighbour, Dave Digger, 41, arrived by chance and helped chase croc off. Dogs turned up, unharmed.

4 Write your own news article about the crocodile incident following the conventions you have learned about. You can add any further details that you wish.

Checklist for success

✔ Write a quick plan for your article of about 4–5 paragraphs.

✔ Decide which paragraph would be best for each of the notes you have taken.

✔ Remember that the key facts always come first.

✔ Check your tenses, as you may need to change tense towards the end.

✔ Choose an appropriate headline.

Check your progress

Some progress

I can adapt what I have read in one form and use the information in a different way.

Good progress

I can adapt specific features from a text appropriately for a new form or purpose.

Excellent progress

I can transform both notes and whole texts into new text types with different purposes.

Adapt the formality of your writing to match the purpose and task

Learning objective

• select the right level of formality for a specific text.

It is important to be able to judge how formal or informal a text should be, and to know how to adapt your writing so that it is appropriate for the reader or audience.

Getting you thinking

Read this extract from the transcript of an interview about the **culling** of badgers.

Glossary

culling: selectively killing animals for environmental or public health reasons

> **Reporter:**
> So, what's your basic argument against...well... this culling, killing, of badgers to stop TB, because the government, DEFRA, are convinced it's right?

> **Protester:** It's simple. It's not gonna stop TB. There's been loads of research done and most people, well scientists... experts...well they all say that there's no hard evidence culling will work! And we now know that only 6% of badgers have TB so any cull is gonna be pretty hit-and-miss, if you know what I mean. Plus we all know what really causes TB in cattle – it's moving stacks of cows around the country. That's what's to blame if you ask me.

 If you were a reporter who wanted to write this up for a national newspaper, you would need to

- sum up the topic simply and clearly
- report the views of the protester, but remove informal or unnecessary turns of phrase so the article represents their views accurately.

a) Which words or phrases could you omit?

b) Which informal words or phrases would you change?

How does it work?

Most articles dealing with controversial issues try to balance explanation with different opinions. Sometimes this is in the form of *direct quotation*, sometimes in the form of *reported speech*.

past tense used for
reports of what was said

An anonymous protester *argued that* the proposed badger cull
was not *going to prevent* TB.

past tense, and change
from 'gonna stop' to
'going to prevent'

Note that there are no speech marks, nor any reference to
the writer ('I').

Now you try it

2 Read the transcript again, then turn the rest of it into a
formal newspaper report. Use this as a starting point:

> An anonymous protester argued that the
> proposed badger cull was not going to prevent
> TB. He also asserted that extensive research
> had been done and...

You could try to include one direct quotation from the
protester. Decide which one is most suitable.

Apply your skills

The reporter also managed to interview a local farmer. Here is the
transcript of what he said.

> **Alan Rickway:** I mean, it makes my blood boil! These
> people...I mean, they don't have to deal with losing half
> your herd, like I did this winter. We've got to do something.
> I mean, this crazy idea that it's all to do with moving cattle
> about all over the country – well, that's just nuts! I reared
> my cattle here, on the farm, and they're slaughtered locally.
> We do things by the book, so you tell me how TB got
> into my herd!

3 Note down

   a) the key points the farmer makes

   b) which informal words and phrases you would remove.

4 Write up the farmer's interview as the next part of the
article, using a mix of direct and reported speech. Consider
how you could use the passive voice to make your writing
sound less personal. For example, 'I reared my cattle here'
becomes, 'His cattle *have been reared* on his farm'.

Check your progress

Some progress

I can recognise informal and
formal usages in texts, and use
some of them in my own work.

Good progress

I can adapt an informal text,
changing most informal
features into formal ones,
including reported speech.

Excellent progress

I can take an informal text and
summarise key points, adapt
informal features and move
fluently between direct and
reported speech.

Check your progress

Some progress

- [ ] I can make the purpose of a poem clear through the writing I choose.
- [ ] I can include some travel writing conventions in my own travel writing.
- [ ] I can maintain my viewpoint in persuasive texts, and use some persuasive techniques.
- [ ] I can adapt what I have read in one form and use the information in a different way.
- [ ] I can recognise informal and formal usages in texts, and use some of them in my own work.

Good progress

- [ ] I can use an appropriate form and choose the right language to suit the purpose of a poem.
- [ ] I can use a range of different conventions to create a believable travel account.
- [ ] I can engage the reader and use persuasive techniques to get a response when arguing a case.
- [ ] I can adapt specific features from a text appropriately for a new form or purpose.
- [ ] I can adapt an informal text, changing most informal features into formal ones, including reported speech.

Excellent progress

- [ ] I can write poetry using a range of literary devices and techniques to match purpose and tone.
- [ ] I can carefully select from a variety of techniques to create a convincing and exciting account.
- [ ] I can sustain my viewpoint using subtle and more direct techniques to persuade the reader.
- [ ] I can transform both notes and whole texts into new text-types with different purposes.
- [ ] I can take an informal text and summarise key points, adapt informal features and move fluently between direct and reported speech.

3

Chapter 3
Organise and present whole texts effectively

What's it all about?

You need to structure your ideas effectively to ensure that your writing has maximum impact.

This chapter will show you how to

- effectively control and sequence your work, thinking about the reader's reaction

- summarise and organise material from different sources

- use a range of features to signal the text's direction to the reader

- develop clear and effective introductions

- manage information, ideas and events to maximise the effect on the reader.

Effectively control and sequence your work, thinking about the reader's reaction

Learning objectives

- structure your work effectively
- write to achieve your desired audience reaction.

Whatever genre you are writing in, you should be thinking carefully about the effect you want your writing to have on your audience.

Getting you thinking

Read these scenes from the opening of a play called *Stone Cold*.

Scene 1

The street. A litter bin. A yellow spot comes up on Link. He looks bored. His clothes are scruffy and he looks dirty. He takes a good look at the audience, then speaks to them.

LINK   Have you ever sat and watched people, really watched them? They're all in their own little world. Now and then they'll let you in if they're feeling brave or if they think they know you. But the rest of the time you might as well be invisible.

A couple of passers-by walk right in front of him. One drops a crisp packet at his feet.

　　　See what I mean?

Link picks up the crisp packet to see if there's anything left inside. There isn't. He moves towards the litter bin. The lights fade.

Scene 2

Shelter's living room. There is an armchair, small table, standard lamp and fireplace. A doorway leads from this room to the bathroom and kitchen. There is a window with heavy, drawn curtains. A cat lies quietly in a basket in front of the fireplace. Above is hung a portrait of an old-looking soldier. Shelter enters with a bowl of tomato soup.

SHELTER   *(thinking out loud)* Haven?…Home… House…

He sits down, puts his soup on the table and picks up a dictaphone and starts to record.

> Day one. Everything is ready. Practice mission executed successfully. Executed. *(Sniggers. There's a knock at the door. Shelter ignores it).* Only complaint at present time is constant pestering from man upstairs. Have now verified code name and will shortly post mission statement to relevant body. Operation to be known as...

He stops the tape for time to think. He ignores another knock at the door.

> Hostel?...Shack...Shed...

Another knock. He is slightly riled.

> Shelter! That's it. *(recording it)* Operation Shelter! Perfect. Succinct, yet welcoming.

Switches the tape off and slurps a mouthful of soup. There's another knock. The soup drips from his mouth as he speaks.

> Get. Lost.

Stone Cold by Joe Standerline (based on the novel by Robert Swindells)

1 How does the playwright want us to feel about Link in the opening scene?

2 How does he establish Link's relationship with the audience?

3 How does he want us to feel about Shelter? How can you tell?

4 Think about the structure of the two scenes. How does the order in which they are presented – Link, then Shelter – affect the way we see the two characters?

How does it work?

Structure is all about how you choose to present ideas. The audience's reactions are affected by the order in which you reveal information.

In plays, some information is given through actions and appearance rather than words alone. There are conventions for how to include this information in a script:

- *how a character speaks* should be shown in brackets after the character's name – as in (*thinking out loud*) and (*recording it*) above. These instructions help the actors work out how to say their lines.

- *what characters do onstage* can come either in brackets or in a separate paragraph – when the action belongs to one character and/or is acted out during that one speech, it is better in the brackets.

Descriptions of setting and characters' appearance are usually given in a paragraph of stage directions, often at the start of a scene.

> **Top tip**
>
> All stage directions are written in the present tense. This is because what they describe is happening as we read or watch the play.

Now you try it

You are going to write two connecting scenes for a play about the dangers of unhealthy living for teenagers.

 5 First plan how you will structure the scenes. Here are two possible ways you could open the play:

Structure 1

Scene 1: a lazy teenager lying in front of the TV eating junk food.
On the other side of the stage, lights up on Scene 2: another teenager at a table eating a salad and reading a book.

Structure 2

Scene 1: a plump, middle-aged jogger, Big Joe, runs on to the stage puffing and then leans heavily on a railing. He pulls out a packet of cigarettes and is about to light one. At that moment, a teenager, Young Joe – in fact, the man as a boy, thirty years or so earlier – comes up to him.

Young Joe: You don't wanna do that.

Big Joe: What's it to you, sunshine?

On your own, decide which of these structures has the best potential. You could also think of a different structure that might work better.

---

6 Next, think carefully about how you want your audience to respond to the characters. For each character, decide

a) what he or she says

b) how he or she says it, and what his or her voice is like

c) what he or she is wearing

d) what he or she does onstage

e) what the setting is like

f) how you want the audience to feel about the character.

> **Top tip**
>
> Your actors have to speak all of their lines aloud (or even learn them) so don't waffle. If in doubt, cut it out.

7 Then, draft the first two scenes of the play. As you draft your play, keep a log-book of your decisions, such as:

a) why you have chosen to write the scenes as you have done

b) what you have revealed about each character, and when (did you hold back information? Did you keep the audience guessing? Did you use contrasting scenes or ideas, as in *Stone Cold*?)

At this stage you are still trying things out to make sure your scenes present the story you want. Don't be afraid to change things that aren't working: for instance, you may decide to change Big Joe to Big Jolene or to make Big Joe sadder or to make the whole play funny. Cut lines that don't help your storyline or argument.

Apply your skills

8 Share your script ideas with a small group. Explain how you have structured your drama, and how you have tried to get your message across.

9 If time allows, choose one or two of the dramas in your group and perform them.

10 Ask your audience to tell you how they responded to the characters, and why. Was this what you were expecting? If not, how could you get them to react the way you want?

11 Write down these thoughts and *redraft* your work. This is probably the most important stage, as you can pinpoint what really made an impact on the audience, and adjust or cut anything that didn't work.

Check your progress

Some progress »
I can structure my work clearly.

Good progress »»
I can control and organise my work, thinking about the audience's reaction.

Excellent progress »»»
I can skilfully manage information, ideas and events to elicit an audience reaction.

Summarise and organise material from different sources

Learning objectives

- list relevant information from two sources
- organise facts and figures into an argument.

It is important to know how to select and write up relevant information into a clear summary.

Getting you thinking

Read these two newspaper articles about the homeless.

Homeless crisis as 400 youths a day face life on the streets of Britain

Number sleeping rough in London since April already up by 32% on whole of last year

A major study revealed today by the *Sunday Mirror* found 13,000 youngsters went to local authorities in October to declare themselves homeless or seek advice on how to cope.

And the number sleeping rough in London alone since April is already up by 32 per cent on the whole of last year.

The survey of more than 500 charities and councils around the country found support workers can barely cope with the huge rise in homeless youngsters [...].

The grim findings are expected to be backed up in the latest Government figures – already showing a 15 per cent rise in youth homelessness – out this week.

Pressures

But the true extent of the problem is likely to be even worse because many rough sleepers will never seek help.

Young homeless people told the *Sunday Mirror* the problem often starts because of their difficulty in finding regular work in the economic downturn.

Last month unemployment in the 16–24 group hit a million and the number of NEETs (not in education, employment or training) reached 1.16 million [...].

The report found family breakdown, often linked to financial pressures, is the main cause of young people leaving home and having to sleep rough.

The *Mirror*, 4 December 2011

'Bob the cat rescued me...'

James Bowen says beloved feline friend helped him go from a nobody to a somebody – and he's now the subject of an international bestseller

He's Bob The Street Cat, subject of an international bestseller and about to make his first foray into Hollywood movies in the film of his own eventful little life [...].

1 The book *A Street Cat Named Bob* and sequel *The World According To Bob*, out this week, were written by Bob's human, 33-year-old James Bowen.

In pairs, read the 'crisis' article, paragraph by paragraph. Make notes in two columns titled 'What is the homelessness crisis?' and 'What are the causes of the crisis?'

2 What two pieces of information in the second article support the argument that, despite James's individual good fortune, homelessness is generally a serious problem? Add this information to your notes.

How does it work?

Every paragraph in the first article is relevant to your notes about the homelessness crisis, but not every *word* is. You can *paraphrase* and leave words out.

Although homelessness is not the focus of the second story, relevant information about the issue is still included.

James had been homeless for more than a decade when he found stray, injured Bob.

The inspiring tail (!) of their unlikely friendship has now sold 750,000 copies in the UK alone, and been translated into 27 languages.

As James tells it: 'Our story seemed to connect with people who were facing difficult times in their lives.'

Polly Hudson, *The Mirror*, 1 July 2013

Now you try it

3 Re-read the inspiring story about Bob and James. List (in note form) three *facts* or *figures* that make James a 'somebody' now.

Apply your skills

4 An MP suggests that all homeless people need to do is show initiative, quoting your three facts and figures about James. Write an argument essay for your school magazine summarising James's experience (in one paragraph) and explaining why the MP is wrong (in five paragraphs, using all the facts and figures that you have gathered). Call your essay 'One chance in 1.16 million'.

Check your progress

Some progress 〉〉
I can select relevant information from a text.

Good progress 〉〉
I can collect together relevant information to create and sustain a line of argument in my writing.

Excellent progress 〉〉〉
I can carefully select facts, figures and relevant details to support a convincing argument.

Use a range of features to signal the text's direction to the reader

Learning objectives

- use writing techniques to help the reader understand what your purpose is
- use structural devices in your writing.

When you write, it is important to use language and structure to steer your audience in the direction you want them to go. Speeches are often written with the clear intention of making an audience react in a certain way. To do this, the speech must use techniques to direct the audience.

Getting you thinking

Read aloud this extract from Earl Spencer's speech at the funeral of his sister, Princess Diana.

> I stand before you today, the representative of a family in grief, in a country in mourning, before a world in shock.
>
> We are all united, not only in our desire to pay our respects to Diana, but rather in our need to do so, because such was her extraordinary appeal that the tens of millions of people taking part in this service all over the world via television and radio who never actually met her feel that they too lost someone close to them in the early hours of Sunday morning.
>
> It is a more remarkable tribute to Diana than I can ever hope to offer to her today.
>
> Diana was the very essence of compassion, of duty, of style, of beauty. All over the world she was the symbol of selfless humanity. A standard bearer for the rights of the truly downtrodden. A very British girl who transcended nationality. Someone with a natural nobility who was classless and who proved in the last year that she needed no royal title to continue to generate her particular brand of magic.
>
> Today is our chance to say 'thank you' for the way you brightened our lives, even though God granted you but half a life. We will all feel cheated always that you were taken from us so young and yet we must learn to be grateful that you came at all.

1 What techniques does Earl Spencer use to make an impact on his audience?

2 How is he trying to make us think or feel about Diana?

3 What is the topic or purpose of each paragraph?

How does it work?

Earl Spencer makes it clear to the audience that Princess Diana is the subject of his speech: he mentions her name many times.

The opening paragraph is a *sentence in four parts*. It is a *list* that builds outwards from him to his family, to the country and finally the world. It draws together his personal grief with that of his listeners.

He moves from talking about himself ('*I*') in the first paragraph, to talking collectively about what '*We*' feel in the second paragraph. Finally, in the last paragraph he talks directly to Diana as '*you*' – a technique that adds emotional power.

The paragraphs are generally quite *short,* and each one has a *clear focus*. In paragraph four, Earl Spencer signals the topic of his paragraph clearly – 'Diana was the very essence of compassion, of duty, of style, of beauty' – before elaborating on this statement.

Now you try it

You are trying to get your class to vote for you in a school election. You need to write a speech explaining why they should pick you.

4 First, plan your speech. What persuasive techniques can you use? Think about

- addressing your audience directly as 'you'
- using lists (especially lists of three)
- using personal pronouns such as 'I' and 'we'.

5 Now think about the structure of your speech.

a) Will you begin by talking about yourself, then explain what you will change at school? Or will you begin with the issues and move on to your role at the end?

b) How can you build your speech to a climactic moment?

Remember to anticipate some of the questions that might be asked by your audience.

Apply your skills

6 Give your speech. Take feedback from your group on what kind of impact it made on them and how it could be improved.

Check your progress

Some progress

I can link my paragraphs together to indicate the overall direction of a speech.

Good progress

I can use a range of features to signal the direction of a speech to the audience.

Excellent progress

I can use a variety of devices to influence the audience's response to my speech.

Develop clear and effective introductions

Learning objective

- write a clear, effective and engaging introduction.

The introduction to a piece of writing signals to the reader what you are writing about. Different styles of writing require different types of introduction.

Getting you thinking

Look at the following opening of a novel.

> I am afraid.
>
> Someone is coming.
>
> That is, I think someone is coming, though I am not sure, and I pray that I am wrong. I went into the church and prayed all this morning. I sprinkled water in front of the altar, and put some flowers on it, violets and dogwood.
>
> But there is smoke. For three days there has been smoke, not like the time before. That time, last year, it rose in a great cloud a long way away, and stayed in the sky for two weeks. A forest fire in the dead woods, and then it rained and the smoke stopped. But this time it is a thin column, like a pole, not very high.
>
> And the column has come three times, each time in the late afternoon. At night I cannot see it, and in the morning, it is gone. But each afternoon it comes again, and it is nearer. At first it was behind Claypole Ridge, and I could see only the top of it, the smallest smudge. I thought it was a cloud, except that it was too grey, the wrong colour, and then I thought: there are no clouds anywhere else. I got the binoculars and saw that it was narrow and straight; it was smoke from a small fire. When we used to go in the truck, Claypole Ridge was fifteen miles, though it looks closer, and the smoke was coming from behind that.
>
> Beyond Claypole Ridge there is Ogdentown, about ten miles further. But there is no one left alive in Ogdentown.
>
> *Z for Zachariah* by Robert C. O'Brien

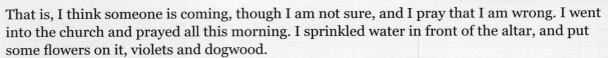

1 What makes this an effective opening?

2 What information does Robert C. O'Brien give the reader at the start?

3 Why do you think he chooses to give this information then?

4 What information is *withheld* until the very end of the extract?

How does it work?

Explanations of the uneasiness behind the first two one-sentence paragraphs gradually emerge, but even the 'reveal' at the end makes us want to know more. The writer gives us just enough information at every stage to want to read on.

Now you try it

Compare this with the top half of a web page. Like any text, it aims to engage your attention, but how is it different from a story opening?

3 .4

> **Top tip**
>
> Remember to withhold some information to keep the reader interested.

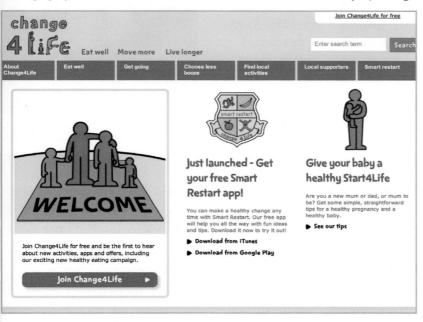

5 Discuss with a partner:

a) Where does the text begin? Who decides – you (as the reader) or the website designer? How?

b) How does the text engage your attention?

c) Does it have any similarities with the novel opening?

Apply your skills

6 Imagine you have been left alone, isolated in your town after a devastating attack or disease that has left everyone nearby dead. Plan your own opening to a piece of creative writing in which you tell your story. You should reveal some details of: who you are, where the events took place, what happened to the other people, how you survived and what happened to you.

Consider how the opening attracts or engages readers.

Check your progress

Some progress

I can plan a clear opening to a piece of creative writing.

Good progress

I can write clear opening paragraphs that introduce themes clearly.

Excellent progress

I can skilfully control the openings of my writing to influence the reader's response.

Manage information, ideas and events to maximise the effect on the reader

Learning objectives

- organise your writing to make the maximum impact on your reader
- write an effective newspaper article.

It is very important to keep your audience in mind throughout a piece of writing. Journalists often write with a clear viewpoint, which they want you to share. They tailor their language, structure and writing style to their typical reader – for example, tabloids (like *The Sun*) tend to use simpler, more direct language for readers who want 'bite-sized' chunks of news and information.

Getting you thinking

Read the following newspaper article.

I'm selfie harming

Emma Power posts up to 20 snaps of herself online a DAY – and feels physically SICK if she can't.

The self-confessed selfie-addict often spends HOURS posing for up to 60 shots and constantly checks her smartphone to see what others think of the pictures she uploads.

The 19 year old is a hardcore example of a new trend in which people take pictures of themselves and post them on social media websites.

Initially, Emma thought it would be a fun way to show off that day's look – but now she won't even go out until she gets a good reaction from people viewing her pictures…

'It sounds silly but I need them to feel good about myself.'

'While celebrities continue to post selfies, I will too.'

The Sun, 12 September 2013

---

1 How does *The Sun* get its message over to its audience?

What do you notice about the use of

- words chosen
- paragraphs
- the order of information
- an ending linking back to the beginning
- italics
- capital letters
- quotations
- headline

How does it work?

This is an article in a tabloid newspaper, It tightly packs lots of information into a small number of words and gets its message across in a bold, simple, **emotive** way. All the stylistic features of the article – words, paragraph type and so on – are easy to understand and immediately engaging.

Glossary

emotive: able to provoke strong emotions

Now you try it

2 Use the list of features in Activity 1 to compare this article from the broadsheet newspaper *The Guardian* to the article from *The Sun*. The article from *The Guardian* also describes a teenager's concerns about her identity. Think about the way *The Guardian* manages the information and how its 'broadsheet' stylistic features help the writer talk about her subject.

The last laugh

Malala Yousafzai says she's lost herself. 'In Swat (district) I studied at the same school for 10 years and there I was just considered to be Malala. Here I'm famous, here people think of me as the girl who was shot by the Taliban. The real Malala has gone somewhere and I can't find her.'

We are sitting in a boardroom on the seventh floor of the new Birmingham library, the glass walls allowing us a view of a city draped in mist, a sharp contrast to the 'paradise' of Swat, with its tall mountains and clear rivers which Malala recalls wistfully. It should be desperately sad but the world's most famous 16-year-old makes it difficult for you to feel sorry for her. In part, it is the way she is so poised ... But more than that, it is to do with how much of the conversation is punctuated by laughter.

Kamila Shamsie, *The Guardian*, 8 October 2013

3 In groups of four, plan an article for your school newspaper about a current issue that is important to your peer group. This could be: teenagers in the news, a new sports hall/ sports event, school dinners, students cheating in a test or winning a prize.

Discuss whether you would choose a tabloid or broadsheet format. What would your headline be?

Apply your skills

4 Write the article you have planned, in your own preferred format. Remember to use the conventions of that format for maximum effect.

Check your progress

Some progress

I can clearly organise my writing into appropriate paragraphs across the whole text.

Good progress

I can control and sequence events and ideas, taking account of the reader's reaction.

Excellent progress

I can skilfully shape information, ideas and events to achieve my intended purpose and effect.

Check your progress

Some progress

- [ ] I can structure my work clearly.
- [ ] I can develop my material across the whole piece of writing.
- [ ] I can develop clear links between my paragraphs.
- [ ] I can make my ending link back to my opening.
- [ ] I can organise information into logical paragraphs.
- [ ] I can organise a dramatic text into stage directions and speeches.

Good progress

- [ ] I can skilfully control the organisation of my writing.
- [ ] I can write with a specific reader or audience in mind.
- [ ] I can use opening paragraphs to introduce themes clearly according to my form.
- [ ] I can use linking devices between paragraphs.
- [ ] I can organise information into effective paragraphs.
- [ ] I can organise a dramatic text into effective stage directions and speeches.

Excellent progress

- [ ] I can skilfully manage and shape information, ideas and events.
- [ ] I can use introductions to influence a reader's response.
- [ ] I can develop characters, plots, events and arguments clearly throughout the whole piece.
- [ ] I can use a variety of devices to influence the reader's thoughts and feelings.
- [ ] I can skilfully control how much information to give the reader and exactly when to do this.
- [ ] I can organise a dramatic text into convincing stage directions and speeches.

4

Chapter 4
Construct paragraphs and use cohesion

What's it all about?

It is important to use paragraphs effectively in your writing, thinking about how their structure increases the impact of the content.

This chapter will show you how to

- structure a fiction paragraph for effect
- decide how and where to start a new paragraph
- create cohesion in non-fiction
- write cohesively for a purpose
- shape ideas into cohesive paragraphs.

Structure a fiction paragraph for effect

Learning objective

- structure the supply of information in a fiction paragraph.

Structuring your paragraphs carefully can control the flow of information and add interest to your fiction writing.

Getting you thinking

Look at this opening paragraph from a 19th-century short story.

Isa Whitney, brother of the late Elias Whitney, D.D., Principal of the Theological College of St George's, was much addicted to opium. The habit grew upon him, as I understand, from some foolish freak when he was at college, for having read **De Quincey**'s description of his dreams and sensations, he had drenched his tobacco with **laudanum** in an attempt to produce the same effects. He found, as so many more have done, that the practice is easier to attain than to get rid of, and for many years he continued to be a slave to the drug, an object of mingled horror and pity to his friends and relatives. I can see him now, with yellow, pasty face, drooping lids and pin-point pupils, all huddled in a chair, the wreck and ruin of a noble man.

'The Man with the Twisted Lip' by Arthur Conan Doyle

 1 Where do the two most important pieces of information or description come in this paragraph? Think about

a) when we are given the first pieces of information about Isa Whitney

b) when we see the sad effect of this on his life.

Glossary

De Quincey: author of the autographical book *Confessions of an Opium Eater*

Laudanum: a mixture containing opium that was used as pain relief medicine

How does it work?

The key information – relating to Isa Whitney's addiction and its impact – comes at the end of the long opening sentence and the long final sentence. In fact, the whole description depends on long sentences that build up information and images of Isa Whitney but withhold key information until the end of each sentence.

For example, a shocking list of images is followed by the sad result of this addiction:

I can see him now, with yellow, pasty face, drooping lids and pin-point pupils, all huddled in a chair, the *wreck and ruin of a noble man.*

This long sentence is really just a simple sentence – 'I can see him now' with other phrases adding detailed description.

2 Turn the long sentence on page 52 into four short ones. The first has been done for you.

    a) I can see him now, with his yellow, pasty face.

    b) He had...

    c) He would sit...

    d) He was the...

3 Which version works better? Why?

4 Now try writing your own extended sentences.

    a) Add a shocking piece of information to this factual sentence:

> Our neighbour, Mr Cartwright, 52, a quiet, balding, unassuming man who was deputy manager of a local hardware shop, was also a_____.

    b) Build a list of shocking images followed by the result:

> After he'd left, I could just make out his wife's shape, slumped in her wheelchair, in the rain-streaked conservatory, smoking endless cigarettes, a _____ and _____ woman.

Apply your skills

5 Continue with Mr Cartwright and his wheelchair-bound wife, or invent your own characters. Create an opening paragraph for a story in which you

    a) start with a plain, factual description of someone and then add a surprise revelation

    b) develop some background information, which tells us more about the person and their situation

    c) finish with a powerful image or images and an observation about this person's character, life or situation.

Check your progress

Some progress
I can write a paragraph about a fictional character.

Good progress
I can structure an effective opening paragraph giving the reader information about a character.

Excellent progress
I can structure a vivid opening paragraph using powerful images to construct a fictional character.

Decide how and where to start a new paragraph

Learning objectives

- understand how and where to start paragraphs
- vary paragraph length for effect.

Sometimes a long paragraph piling up details about a particular topic or point can make a real impact. At other times, a short, single-sentence paragraph can draw attention to an important idea.

Getting you thinking

Look at the *monologue* below. Charles Dickens is addressing an audience.

> Welcome ladies and gentlemen, welcome! I shall be most pleased to tell you something of my life.
>
> I was born in 1812, the year Napoleon invaded Russia. A cold, harsh winter it was, a winter that saw the French army **decimated** and the great Napoleon's men reduced to traipsing through the cruel snows of Russia, hoping to find their way back to France. But enough of that, it was the year that gave birth to me – a winter of note! My early years were as harsh as the winter I was born. My father was a debtor. Like Mr Micawber, he was unable to make ends meet and was thrown into a debtor's prison. My parents took me out of school and I was forced to work in a blacking factory. I cannot, even now, describe the agonies I endured there. I thought my life was wasted, my potential squandered by the monotonous, tedious work.
>
> Ladies and gentlemen, that most terrible of experiences gave me my ideas for my poor characters, my imaginary children.
>
> Adapted from *Monologues with Duologue Activities* by Keith West

Charles Dickens.

Glossary

decimated: completely destroyed

1 The large paragraph can be split into three smaller ones.

   a) Where would you put the paragraph breaks?

   b) What is the **topic sentence** in each of your new paragraphs?

2 What is the effect of the final, single-sentence paragraph?

Glossary

topic sentence: the sentence that explains what a paragraph is mainly about

How does it work?

New paragraphs should mark a change in time, person or subject. Each new start should have an effect – for example, to surprise the reader or introduce a new idea.

When constructing paragraphs, identify the topic sentence in each paragraph and ensure that every sentence relates to it.

Now you try it

Here is an extended monologue that hasn't been organised into paragraphs.

As a street child there are but three places where I can lay my head on Her Majesty's streets. The first is the cold stone of the embankment near Waterloo Bridge. No gas-lamps reach there, nor the long, unfeeling arm of the law. There, I am safe. There, I sleep. There, 'though cold, I have rest. This is not like my second place. I go to Old Brompton cemetery. It is an hour's walk. It is a quiet, secluded place, and I have sleepers for company who neither snore, nor cry, nor prod me awake. Indeed, it is a place I know well for my own dear parents are buried there. Those sleepers have the deepest and warmest beds – the earth… My third place of repose is the Royal Stables… My companions there, gentle dappled mares and respectful stallions, watch over me. They are the only angels in my life.

The Poor, Truthful Life of Hetty Marwood, aged 10½ by Mike Gould

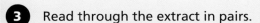

3 Read through the extract in pairs.

   a) Decide how to split the monologue into three or four separate paragraphs.

   b) Identify your topic sentences and see if you can achieve different effects by making your paragraphs different lengths.

> **Top tip**
>
> Paragraphs don't have to be the same length. An occasional one-line paragraph can have enormous impact.

Apply your skills

4 Draft a monologue from the viewpoint of: a policeman, the cemetery keeper or one of the horses. Do they notice homeless children like Hetty? How do they feel about her?

As a start, plan three or four paragraphs to cover three or four ideas. Then rework the paragraphs to create more impact – for example, by contrasting long and short paragraphs.

5 Now redraft your monologue – are there any sentences that don't relate to the central theme of the paragraph? Can these be moved or cut?

Check your progress

Some progress
I can rearrange the order of sentences within paragraphs.

Good progress
I can rearrange sentences and paragraphs for effect.

Excellent progress
I can rearrange sentences and paragraphs for emphasis, clarity and impact.

Create cohesion in non-fiction

Learning objectives
- write paragraphs with cohesion
- write paragraphs that flow.

When presenting an argument or an account, remember to link your ideas so that they appear in a logical sequence.

Getting you thinking

Read this opinion piece about football managers.

Football is often described as the beautiful game. There have been many exciting moments and memories. But however good the players are, a team cannot do well without a brilliant manager.

There have been many great managers in football but the greatest manager, in my opinion, was Brian Clough.

Greater than Alex Ferguson, Bob Paisley and George Graham? Yes, because Clough did not manage a rich and powerful team like Manchester United, Liverpool or Arsenal – he took over clubs such as Derby and Nottingham Forest. With Clough as manager, both clubs won honours they did not dream of winning before. Neither club has won honours since.

Clough's teams were full of style, flair and they were irrepressible. Under him, Derby County won the League Championship and Nottingham Forest won the European Cup twice. If Clough had managed Manchester United or Arsenal, his teams would have won every honour in sight.

This manager's greatness was to make something out of ordinary players. He turned them into stars! Some part of every player under Clough feared him, some part respected his quickness of mind and another part of a player responded to his encouragement.

1 How does the writer make links between paragraphs?

How does it work?

The end of each paragraph clearly links to the start of the next as ideas are built up and extended. The final paragraph links back to the first.

Cohesion within paragraphs can be improved by the use of linking words (called *conjunctions* or *connectives*). Here are some examples of linking words and phrases:

however	then	finally	meanwhile	equally
in the same way	whereas	instead of	alternatively	although

Cohesion can also be improved by repeating key words, and by replacing key words with *pronouns* to refer back (Brian Clough, Clough, the manager, he).

Look at the newspaper report below. The journalist knows that Bernard Sheepshanks, the newspaper's editor, will not be happy with her work. In desperation, she turns to you for help.

At last, a British woman tennis player to be reckoned with.

Laura Robson is the current no. 1 ranked female player in the United Kingdom. She was born on 21 January 1994 in Melbourne. She moved to the UK aged 6. She won the Wimbledon Junior Girls' Championship in 2008 aged 14.

As a junior, she also twice reached the final of the girls' singles tournament in 2009 and 2010 at the Australian Open. She won her first professional tournament in November 2008.

She reached a WTA singles rank of 27 in July 2013. Her doubles tour rank on 19 August 2013 was 88. Both of these were career-bests. She won an Olympic doubles silver medal in London 2012 with Andy Murray.

Robson is the first British woman since Samantha Smith to reach the fourth round of a major tournament. Samantha Smith did this at Wimbledon in 1998. Robson followed suit at the US Open in 2012 and at Wimbledon in 2013.

She was named WTA Newcomer of the Year for 2012.

2 Develop the article for the journalist, so that old Sheepshanks will be pleased. You will need to add and alter paragraphs and create cohesion with linking words, repeated words and pronouns.

Apply your skills

3 Produce your own piece of non-fiction writing.

Either:

a) Research and write a short essay about the person you think is a brilliant manager of a sports team.

Or:

b) Write about a great teacher who has motivated you.

Make sure your paragraphs are linked and that there is a logic to their order.

Check your progress

Some progress »

I can link my paragraphs.

Good progress »»

I can create cohesion between and within paragraphs.

Excellent progress »»»

I can create cohesion across the whole text.

Write cohesively for a purpose

Learning objective

• use language devices to improve the cohesion of your writing.

You can use repetition and linking words and phrases connect your sentences and paragraphs and create a cohesive, effective piece of writing.

Getting you thinking

1 Look at this description of bees at work by a modern science writer. How well does he link his paragraphs together?

> Honey bees don't have ears, but they are exquisitely sensitive to vibrations which they receive through their legs…
>
> Bees are known to use vibrations to communicate with each other in their hives and scientists have already been able to decode a particular behaviour known as a waggle dance, which the bees use to tell others about the location of good food sources.
>
> In the waggle dance, a bee will beat its wings rapidly and shake its body from side to side as it walks in a single direction along the honeycomb before circling back and starting the dance again. The duration and direction of the dance tells other bees where the flowers are.
>
> Richard Gray, *Daily Telegraph*, 24 March 2013

How does it work?

The paragraphs repeat 'bees' and 'waggle dance', referring us back to ideas already stated.

Now you try it

It is important to make your sentences and paragraphs cohesive and effective for your *purpose*. Look at this table of *connectives*.

Purpose	Connectives
Adding	as well as, besides, also
Cause and effect	therefore, thus, consequently, as a result of
Sequencing	first, second, third, next, then, after
Contrasting	whereas, otherwise, unlike, on the other hand, in contrast
Qualifying	however, although, unless, except, if, as long as, apart from, yet, despite
Emphasising	above all, in particular, especially, significantly, indeed, notably, most of all
Illustrating	for example, in the case of
Comparing	similarly, likewise, as with, like, compared with

2 In pairs, explain to your partner how to put up a tent or get to a campsite (without satnav!) using all the sequencing connectives in the table *at least once*.

3 Role-play a discussion about the pros and cons of outdoor holidays. See if, between you, you can use all the *qualifying* and *emphasising* connectives. They are ideal for putting forward a balanced argument.

Apply your skills

Now read this further extract on bees.

Bees pollinate more than £1 billion worth of crops in the UK each year, including cabbages, sprouts, cauliflowers, carrots, strawberries, apples and pears. Many wild flowers and garden flowers also rely upon the insects to spread their pollen.

In recent years bee keepers have reported increased losses through the winter months.

Increased pesticide use and pollution has also been blamed for weakening bee colonies and leaving them more vulnerable to disease [...].

Richard Gray, *Daily Telegraph*, 24 March 2013

4 Read the opening paragraph below, then add three further paragraphs using the bridges suggested. Use the information from the extract above to help you write the additional paragraphs.

Try to use the connectives listed in the table on page 58 to make your writing cohesive within each sentence and paragraph.

> It has been suggested that bees think and communicate. For instance, they work together on building hives.
>
> Paragraph 2 – In addition,
>
> Paragraph 3 – Furthermore,
>
> Paragraph 4 – In fact,

Check your progress

Some progress 〉
I can write cohesive sentences and paragraphs.

Good progress 〉
I can write cohesive essays.

Excellent progress 〉〉
I can make distinctions about choosing connectives for my purpose.

Shape ideas into cohesive paragraphs

Learning objective

• sharpen the focus of your writing.

Cohesive paragraphs present facts in a *logical* and *focused* way. It is important to ensure that your ideas are well connected throughout your writing, and lead naturally to your conclusion.

Getting you thinking

 Read the following report. As you do so, consider

a) who has written the report

b) who it is for (the audience)

c) what its purpose is.

A report on our form room, E12

This report has been prepared in response to the request from Mr Wright, Head of Year 9. It considers the state of our form room, E12.

Problems concerning E12

As a result of research carried out for this report, it has been discovered that E12 has paint flaking off the walls. The two radiators fail to work and three windows are cracked and in a potentially dangerous condition. There are no curtains and blinds in the room and the video player does not work.

Possible solution

E12 needs a complete makeover.

Recommendations

1 E12 needs redecorating over the summer holidays.

2 The two radiators need immediate attention.

3 Three windowpanes need replacing.

4 All window areas need curtains.

5 The video player needs replacing with a DVD player.

Report prepared by Jake Winters, 3 March 2013.

How does it work?

The *purpose* of the report is stated in the first sentence. The introduction tells the reader who requested the report, and why.

The second paragraph is written after the investigation into E12 and tells the reader the *findings* of the investigation.

The third paragraph proposes a *possible course of action*. The fourth paragraph presents the reader with a series of clear, numbered points listing the *specific details* of the proposed action.

Now you try it

Your school's head teacher wants to plan for the future, and has asked you to create a proposal for a 'Chill Zone', where pupils can quietly relax and reflect on work, relationships or problems. He has stated that the 'Chill Zone' should be 'light, quiet and comfortable'.

2 Plan your proposal by suggesting five sections and giving each one a heading. The headings need to match the subject of each section. For example:

> Section 1: The purpose of this report

> Section 2: Why the 'Chill Zone' is needed

Think about how you will shape your ideas into cohesive paragraphs that fit into the five sections.

Apply your skills

3 Research further ideas for your 'Chill Zone' proposal by talking to fellow students and teachers.

Set out your report according to the headings you have planned, and remember to keep your writing focused and cohesive throughout.

Try to use language that sounds professional and includes design vocabulary. For example:

Adjectives to describe the feel and tone of the 'Chill Zone'	bright and cool graphics, imposing steel, overhead beams
Specific words to describe the space and building	interior and exterior, inner, outer, eye-level, parallel, vertical
Verbs to do with the movement of peoplein the space or the relationship between areas	flow, connect, link, blur, merge with, lead to, descend, ascend, swing round
Architectural terms	atrium, dome, cube, zone, partition, wall, corridor

Check your progress

Some progress

I can write a report with some cohesive paragraphs for a particular purpose.

Good progress

I can write a report in cohesive paragraphs, using professional language.

Excellent progress

I can write a report in cohesive paragraphs, using professional language and information gained from researching.

Check your progress

Some progress

- [ ] I can arrange sentences into a paragraph.
- [ ] I can rearrange the order of paragraphs.
- [ ] I can replace key words with pronouns.
- [ ] I can create some cohesion within paragraphs.
- [ ] I can connect paragraphs together.
- [ ] I can sometimes write cohesively for a purpose.

Good progress

- [ ] I can arrange sentences within a paragraph to create an effect.
- [ ] I can rearrange sentences and paragraphs for effect.
- [ ] I can replace key words with pronouns for cohesion.
- [ ] I can write connectively creating cohesion within and between paragraphs.
- [ ] I can create paragraphs unified around a theme or topic.
- [ ] I can write cohesively for a purpose.

Excellent progress

- [ ] I can arrange sentences within a paragraph to create a powerful effect.
- [ ] I can rearrange paragraphs for emphasis, clarity and effect.
- [ ] I can improve cohesion of paragraphs by the repetition of key words and replacing pronouns for effect.
- [ ] I can think and write connectively using a range of cohesive devices.
- [ ] I can write using clarity of logic and unity between paragraphs.
- [ ] I can write cohesively for a purpose and to considerable effect.

Chapter 5

Vary sentences for clarity, purpose and effect and write with technical accuracy of syntax and punctuation

What's it all about?

It is important to learn how to vary your sentences in order to write clearly and effectively and to maintain focus. Learning how to use elements of syntax and punctuation accurately will help you to achieve this.

This chapter will show you how to

- use punctuation creatively
- write expressive and varied sentences in descriptive writing
- shape sentences for effect
- write effective dialogue in stories and scripts
- use rhetorical devices to make an impact
- use formal grammar, including tenses and moods of verbs.

Use punctuation creatively

Learning objective

- use punctuation creatively to add interest and variety to sentences.

Chosen deliberately, punctuation will add interest to your writing.

Getting you thinking

Edward Thomas wrote this poem in 1915 while he was a soldier in the First World War. He remembered a train journey in June 1914, just before the war began. The train had stopped at the Cotswold village of Adlestrop, and Thomas had looked out at the summer scene.

Adlestrop

Yes. I remember Adlestrop –
The name, because one afternoon
Of heat the express-train drew up there
Unwontedly. It was late June.

The steam hissed. Someone cleared
   his throat.
No one left and no one came
On the bare platform. What I saw
Was Adlestrop – only the name

And willows, willow-herb, and grass,
And meadowsweet, and haycocks dry,
No whit less still and lonely fair
Than the high cloudlets in the sky.

And for that minute a blackbird sang
Close by, and round him, mistier,
Farther and farther, all the birds
Of Oxfordshire and Gloucestershire.

Edward Thomas

1 Read the poem, looking at the punctuation.

a) First consider *full stops* and *dashes*. Thomas builds silence into his poem by using punctuation to create heavy pauses. Why do you think he introduces the pauses here?

b) Look at the *commas* in the third stanza. In this list, the narrator's view shifts from close-up to long-distance. Where else does Thomas use commas to create this effect?

c) 'Yes' in line one is followed by a full stop. In some versions, there is a comma. Which do you think is better? Why?

Glossary

Unwontedly: in an unusual way

No whit: not a bit

How does it work?

Here is a reminder of the main points of punctuation.

Full stop	.	Marks a major pause, especially at the end of a sentence
Comma	,	Marks a pause in a sentence, separates parts in a list, isolates clauses and phrases, introduces or concludes direct speech
Question mark	?	Indicates a direct question

Exclamation mark	!	Shows that the preceding words contain a shock/surprise or a strong emotion
Apostrophe	'	Indicates a missing letter in a short form ('didn't') and is used to show possession ('Clare's words')
Colon	:	Introduces phrases, clauses or a list
Semicolon	;	Divides balanced statements in a sentence, or longer items in a list
Speech marks	'…' or "…"	Encloses direct speech, and indicates quotations and titles
Ellipsis/dash	… or –	Marks a sudden break in meaning, and a dash can replace a colon
Brackets/paired dashes	( ) or –…–	Marks an additional note within a sentence, slightly set apart from the rest of it

Now you try it

2 Rewrite the paragraph below as a poem, adding punctuation for clarification and effect.

> I recall the factory dark smog and dismal
> shadows the angry roar of engines voices crying
> out in pain small children pale as milk I see dust
> and ash yet through a window a bright moon rising

Apply your skills

'George Eliot' (real name Marian Evans) was brought up in the Warwickshire countryside in the 19th century. She lovingly recalled this landscape in her novel *Middlemarch*.

> Little details gave each field a particular **physiognomy**, dear to the eyes that have looked on them from childhood: the pool in the corner where the grasses were dank and trees leaned whisperingly; the great oak shadowing a bare place in mid-pasture; the huddled ricks and roofs of the homestead; the grey gate and fences against the depths of the bordering wood; and the stray hovel, its old, old thatch full of mossy hills and valleys.

3 Think of a place that means a lot to you and write a descriptive paragraph. Start by using Eliot's pattern: an introductory sentence ending with a colon, followed by a list of remembered details about your place. Divide these details with semicolons and be as precise – and creative – as possible.

Glossary

physiognomy: face, appearance or personality

Check your progress

Some progress

I can use punctuation effectively to make my meaning clear.

Good progress

I can use a full range of punctuation accurately.

Excellent progress

I can use a full range of punctuation confidently and expressively.

Write expressive and varied sentences in descriptive writing

Learning objective

- use a range of sentence forms and features to create exciting narratives and descriptions.

A mixture of long and short sentences is a good way to make descriptions more exciting. Varied sentence features will also help to maximise the effect.

Getting you thinking

A student has tried to write her own ghost story based on a scene from the film *The Turn of the Screw*. In the scene, a ghost appears on a tower of the great house where the young woman narrator works as a governess.

> She came out of the wood. It was evening. Shadows spread across the lawns. The sun lit up the tree tops. Rooks were calling. Then it went quiet. She saw a figure on the tower. It was dark against the sunset. It seemed to stare at her. A chill ran down her spine. She walked on towards the house. The figure moved around the battlements of the tower. It still looked fixedly at her. There was nobody in sight. She ran to get to the nearest door.
>
> The clamour of the rooks returned. Someone was chopping wood. A servant was singing inside the house. She looked back. The figure was gone.

The sentences are very short and repetitive.

 With a partner, discuss how you could run sentences together to make a smoother narrative. The first three have been done for you as an example.

> It was evening as she came out of the wood. Shadows spread across the lawns although the sun still lit up the tree tops. Rooks were calling but suddenly everything went quiet ...

How does it work?

The story's style can be improved by developing some (or most) of the short statements into longer **compound** or **complex sentences**.

Below are some of the most useful sentence structures to try out:

- A *fronted adverbial* is a single adverb or a phrase acting like an adverb, useful for starting sentences:

  then   however   by contrast   finally   similarly

  furthermore   by the lake   after an hour

- A *subordinate clause* can act as an adjective, noun or adverb:

  - *Adjectival* clauses act like an adjective:

    I admired Monet's painting, *which was one of his last works* (adjectival clause describing the painting)

  - *Noun clauses* act like single-word nouns:

    That he completed this picture seems amazing

  - *adverbial clauses* act like adverbs:

    He worked on it *while he underwent eye surgery* (adverbial clause describing 'worked').

These clauses may be placed at the *start*, in the *middle* or at the *end* of a sentence. Their placement depends on where you want the main verb to have the most impact.

Now you try it

In Susan Hill's ghost story, *The Woman in Black*, Arthur Kipps is haunted by a sinister woman dressed in black Victorian clothes. At the end of the story, Kipps hopes he has escaped the woman, but she reappears.

> And then, quite suddenly, I saw her. She was standing away from any of the people, close up to the trunk of one of the trees. I looked directly at her and she at me. There was no mistake. My eyes were not deceiving me. It was she, the woman in black with the wasted face, the ghost of Jennet Humfrye. For a second, I simply stared in incredulity and astonishment, then in cold fear.

compound sentence

simple sentence

Glossary

compound sentences: clauses of equal importance are joined by co-ordinating conjunctions (and, but, or); for example, 'someone was chopping wood *and* a servant was singing inside the house'.

complex sentences: extra details are added to a main clause or simple sentence stem; for example, '*shadows spread across the lawns* although the sun still lit up the tree tops'.

Top tip

Remember, a clause contains a subject and a verb; a phrase may contain a noun or a verb but it does not have a noun doing a verb. A phrase does not make sense as a full sentence in its own right.

2 With a partner, read alternate sentences of the passage on page 67.

a) Look at the first sentence. What is the key idea here? Why are two *phrases* placed before it?

b) Look at the sixth sentence. What is the main idea here? Why are two *phrases* added after it?

c) What is the effect of using both short sentences and longer ones?

Arthur Kipps had first seen the ghost in a churchyard during a funeral. Read the extract below, which describes this moment.

I half-turned, discreetly, and caught a glimpse of another mourner, a woman, who must have slipped into the church after we of the funeral party had taken our places and who stood several rows behind and quite alone, very erect and still, and not holding a prayer book. She was dressed in deepest black, in the style of full mourning that had rather gone out of fashion . . . Indeed, it had clearly been dug out of some old trunk or wardrobe, for its blackness was a little rusty-looking. A bonnet-type hat covered her head and shaded her face, but, although I did not stare, even the swift glance I took of the woman showed me enough to recognise that she was suffering from some terrible wasting disease.

3 Analyse some of the complex sentences in the extract above to see how they add detail to the main ideas or clauses. Look for adverbs as well as the three types of subordinate clauses listed on page 67.

Arthur Kipps sees the woman in black again near an empty house on a lonely island. She is standing among some graves beside a ruined chapel. It is a November afternoon at sunset. The only sounds are the seabirds, the waves and the wind.

4 Write four *complex* sentences about this meeting. Here are four main verb units around which you might build the sentences:

a) darkness was falling

b) she stared

c) I saw

d) I was alone.

5 Extend these sentences into a longer piece of writing.

Shape sentences for effect

Learning objective

- vary the shape and structure of your sentences for effect.

The structure, length and word order of your sentences can all be used to produce a particular effect on your reader.

Getting you thinking

Michael MacDonagh, a *Times* reporter, was in London on 4 August 1914 to record the start of the First World War. The German Army had invaded Belgium. To make Germany withdraw or face a declaration of war, Britain sent an ultimatum that ran out at 11 p.m.

> At the approach of the decisive hour of eleven, we returned in our thousands to Whitehall. Then followed the slow and measured strokes of Big Ben proclaiming to London that it was eleven o'clock. We listened in silence. Was he booming out sweet peace and in red slaughter? No statement was made. There was no public proclamation that we were at war. The great crowd rapidly dispersed in all directions, most of them running to get home quickly and as they ran they cried out rather hysterically, 'War!' 'War!' 'War!'

1 How does Michael MacDonagh use different *sentence structures* to recreate the drama of this scene? Discuss the effects of the

   a) short sentences and longer sentences (especially the second and the last)

   b) use of direct speech, exclamations and a question.

How does it work?

Varied sentence lengths and structures (and quoted speech) are effective in reportage (eyewitness journalism) and description. They can help to give details of the scene and convey the sudden shock of events.

Now you try it

2 Think of a dramatic scene. It could be a road accident, a great sporting moment or a birth in your family.

Describe your scene in six lines, using varied sentence patterns. Try to use

- longer sentences to set the scene and provide detail
- short sentences to convey emphasis or shock
- questions or direct speech to express confusion or excitement.

The writer Richard Aldington was a soldier during World War I. In his novel *Death of a Hero*, he describes the horrors of the Western Front. Here, George Winterbourne – the story's hero – explores the battlefield:

> At dawn one morning when it was misty he walked over the top of Hill 91, where probably nobody had been by day since its capture. The ground was a desert of shell-holes and torn rusty wire, and everywhere lay skeletons in steel helmets, still clothed in the rags of sodden khaki or field grey. Here a fleshless hand still clutched a broken rusty rifle; there a gaping, decaying boot showed the thin, knotty foot-bones. Alone in the white curling mist, drifting slowly past like **wraiths** of the slain, with the far-off thunder of drum-fire beating the air, Winterbourne stood in frozen silence and contemplated the last achievements of civilised men.
>
> *Death of a Hero* by Richard Aldington

Glossary

wraiths: ghosts

polemical: argumentative

3 Read through the extract closely, focusing on the grammar.

a) Find the main clause(s) and main verb(s) in each sentence.

b) What extra details about time, place, people or things has been added to each main clause? What is the effect?

c) How does the long last sentence sum up the horror of the battlefield? Why do you think Aldington structured the final sentencein this way?

d) What does the fronted adverbial ('Alone in the white curling mist') with its two extras ('drifting slowly...' and 'with the far-off...') add to the main clauses?

e) What do you find effective in Aldington's description of the battlefield? (Think about word choice as well as sentence structure.)

4 a) Imagine you have been asked to write a piece of **polemical** writing. You have to describe in detail a situation that you feel strongly about, and make your own opinion clear. The situation could be

- a modern war that you have seen on TV or read about
- the death of animals due to hunting or environmental damage
- global warming.

b) Write a paragraph of your polemic, and make sure to

- use fronted clauses and phrases ('Slowly, I realised...')
- vary the word/clause order of your sentences
- include questions
- use short sentences for emphasis or clarity.

Check your progress

Some progress

I can vary sentence lengths and structures to give clarity and emphasis.

Good progress

I can use some simple and complex sentences for effect.

Excellent progress

I can control a variety of simple and complex sentences for purpose and effect.

Write effective dialogue in stories and scripts

Learning objective
- write accurate and exciting dialogue.

Good stories almost always include dialogue. Dialogue tells us about the characters and their relationships, and is an exciting way to move the story on.

Getting you thinking

In the extract below, Eustace is sent the severed hand of his sinister dead uncle. Somehow the hand is alive and escapes from its box. It has one intention: to kill Eustace. He discusses the missing hand with his housekeeper.

> 'What was its colour?' asked Eustace. 'Black?'
>
> 'Oh no, sir; a greyish white. It crept along in a very funny way, sir. I don't think it had a tail.'
>
> 'What did you do then?'
>
> 'I tried to catch it; but it was no use … I think it must have escaped.'
>
> 'And you think it is the animal that's been frightening the maids?'
>
> 'They said it was a hand that they saw … Emma trod on it once at the bottom of the stairs. She thought then it was a half-frozen toad, only white.'
>
> 'The Beast with Five Fingers' by W.F. Harvey

1 With a partner, discuss which words and phrases describe the hand most effectively.

2 Why do you think the writer chose to use dialogue to tell the reader about the sightings of the hand?

How does it work?

People don't tend to speak in full, formal sentences. For dialogue to come alive, remember to use:

- *casual short forms* like 'don't'
- *speech tags* like 'Oh no' or 'Well, sir'
- *ellipses* (…) to show sudden breaks or pauses
- *adverbs* to tell us *how* people speak.

Top tips

Remind yourself of the technical points about speech punctuation:

Use single inverted commas around speech.

Start a new paragraph when there is a new speaker.

Commas, full stops and question marks should usually come inside the speech marks, as in the passage.

3 Two maids at Eustace's house are discussing their experiences of the strange hand (helping with the washing-up, running up curtains, attacking the cat and so on). Write up their conversation. Think about

a) how you can make what they say exciting and frightening

b) the personality each character will have.

Apply your skills

Susan Hill, the author of *The Woman in Black*, handles dialogue brilliantly. After a funeral, Arthur Kipps talks to a local lawyer about the mysterious figure that he saw in the churchyard.

'Tell me, that other woman…' I said as I reached his side. 'I hope she can find her own way home…she looked so dreadfully unwell. Who was she?'

He frowned.

'The young woman with the wasted face,' I urged, 'at the back of the church and then in the graveyard a few yards away from us.'

Mr Jerome stopped dead. He was staring at me.

'A young woman?'

'Yes, yes, with the skin stretched over her bones. I could scarcely bear to look at her…she was tall, she wore a bonnet type of hat…I suppose to try to conceal as much as she could of her face, poor thing.'

For a few seconds, in that quiet, empty lane, in the sunshine, there was such a silence as must have fallen again now inside the church…

Check your progress

4 Think about how the dialogue works.

a) What information is revealed?

b) How does Hill use language, structure and punctuation to create surprise and suspense?

5 Try writing a radio script that adapts and continues the conversation in the extract above. Your script will be made up of dialogue, so it won't have a narrator. How will your script convey the information that the book's narrator gives – for example, the character's thoughts and reactions? (Refer back to the scripts on pages 38–39 to help you.)

Some progress

I can punctuate and set out speech accurately.

Good progress

I can use an expressive range of punctuation and layout options in story dialogue and scripts.

Excellent progress

I can control speech punctuation and layout for varied purposes and effects.

Use rhetorical devices to make an impact

Learning objectives
- shape sentences using antithesis, repetition or balance
- think about the purpose and effect of such sentences.

Rhetorical devices can help you make an impact on your reader, especially in persuasive writing or speeches.

Getting you thinking

Read the opening of this novel about the French Revolution.

> It was the best of times, it was the worst of times, it was the age of wisdom, it was the age of foolishness, it was the season of Light, it was the season of Darkness, it was the spring of hope, it was the winter of despair...
>
> *A Tale of Two Cities* by Charles Dickens

 1 With a partner:

a) Pick out the patterns of three words that are *repeated* throughout to make a *balanced* structure for the ideas.

b) Now find the pairs of words with *opposite meanings* (*antonyms*).

c) What does this sentence structure suggest about the French Revolution?

How does it work?

There are useful technical terms to describe the techniques displayed in the extract above:

- *antithesis* means contrasting ideas
- *repetition* means repeating the same word pattern
- *balance* means setting one idea against a second.

These are called *rhetorical devices*, and they are crucial in *persuasive writing* or *speeches*. They also create rhythms to make your sentences more enjoyable to read.

Other rhetorical devices include *rhetorical questions* that expect a certain answer ('You do want some more cake, don't you?') and *appeals for sympathy or solidarity* ('My fellow Americans').

Glossary

satire: a literary work that uses humour to criticise failings in people and/or societies

Now you try it

In his 1945 **satire**, *Animal Farm*, George Orwell attacked the way in which cunning political leaders use rhetoric to cheat ordinary people.

In his story, animals at a farm overthrow the neglectful owner Mr Jones and set up a new community in which, supposedly, 'All animals are equal'. Soon, however, the selfish pigs claim the best things on the farm (like the milk and apples) for themselves. Squealer, the pig in charge of **propaganda**, explains to the other animals:

> **'Comrades!'** he cried. 'You do not imagine, I hope, that we pigs are doing this in a spirit of selfishness and privilege? Many of us actually dislike milk and apples. I dislike them myself. Our sole object in taking these things is to preserve our health. Milk and apples (this been proved by Science, comrades) contain substances absolutely necessary to the well-being of a pig. We pigs are brainworkers. The whole management and organisation of this farm depend on us. Day and night we are watching over your welfare. It is for your sake that we drink that milk and eat those apples. Do you know what would happen if we pigs failed in our duty? Jones would come back! Yes, Jones would come back! Surely, comrades,' cried Squealer almost pleadingly, skipping from side to side and whisking his tail, 'surely there is no one among you who wants to see Jones come back?'

2 In the speech above, find examples of rhetorical devices such as:

- repetition
- patterns of three
- rhetorical questions
- appeals for sympathy.

3 How does the last sentence work, and why is it an effective conclusion?

Glossary

propaganda: deliberately one-sided information that is made public to promote a certain cause

comrades: friends or associates (term traditionally used by communists to refer to one another)

Apply your skills

4 Write your own persuasive speech *for* or *against* a controversial topic. This could be

- goal line technology
- single-sex schooling.

a) First, plan your *key points*, giving one paragraph to each. Decide which rhetorical devices you will use and where you will place them.

b) Then write up your speech. Try to use punctuation effectively – for example, include *commas* and *semicolons* to create pauses and divide items in a list.

5 Practise reading your speech to a partner, and really try to persuade them to agree with your argument. Ask for their feedback, and use this to redraft and improve your speech.

Check your progress

Some progress

I can pick out rhetorical devices in persuasive writing.

Good progress

I use rhetorical devices in persuasive writing.

Excellent progress

I can use a full range of persuasive devices effectively.

Use formal grammar, including tenses and moods of verbs

Learning objective
- understand the possibilities of tenses and moods of verbs.

We all use tenses and **moods** of verbs easily in speech because we have picked them up in childhood. There are some moods and tenses you may be less familiar with, which are worth exploring to add distinction to your writing.

Getting you thinking

Shakespeare's play *Henry V* is centred on the Anglo-French Battle of Agincourt. The night before the battle, the French knights are impatient for the fighting to begin. One says:

> 'I would it were morning, for **I would fain** be about the ears of the English.'

Here, '*were*' is the *past subjunctive* of the verb 'to be'. Although most people would write 'I wish it *was* morning' in colloquial English, the subjunctive mood is still used in formal English.

The *present subjunctive* is about *wishes, demands* and *recommendations*. It takes the same form as the base form of the verb: 'do', 'be', 'talk'.

I ask that he *cease* to pester me.   (demand)

It is vital that work *be* stopped at once.   (recommendation)

The *past subjunctive* expresses *regret*, *longing* or *doubt*. It uses '*were*' with I and he/she/it.

If only she *were* here today!   (longing)

You talk as if he *were* a kind man.   (doubt)

1 Use these beginnings to create full sentences:

   a) If I were rich, I…

   b) If your mother were here, she…

   c) You wish you were…

Glossary

moods: this concerns how a sentence behaves: as a statement, question, request, command or response. For example, most sentences are in the *declarative mood (statement)* and some are in *interrogative mood (questions)*

I would fain: old-fashioned phrase meaning *I want to*

Top tip

Make sure you use the correct verb form in each case – for instance, you should say 'I did my homework', not 'I done my homework'.

How does it work?

Verbs are about *actions* (doing) or *states* (being).

Tense means the *time* of the verb. The three basic tenses are *past* (I went), *present* (I go) and *future* (I will go).

There are many sub-tenses:

- simple present: It rains
- simple past: It rained
- present progressive: It is raining
- past progressive: It was raining
- present perfect: It has rained
- past perfect: It had rained
- past perfect progressive: It had been raining

Participles such as *raining* (present) and *rained* (past) are only parts of verbs. They need helping verbs (*auxiliaries*) to make them complete.

Now you try it

2 Try writing the simple past and the past participle forms of these verbs:

do	buy	bring	choose	dive	light	sing
build	fight	go	lie	hide	show	write

Apply your skills

A Roman writer called Pliny saw the great eruption of the volcano Vesuvius that buried the towns of Pompeii and Herculaneum in AD 79.

My mother implored, entreated and commanded me to escape as best I could – a young man might escape, whereas she was old and slow and could die in peace as long as she had not been the cause of my death too. I refused to save myself without her, and grasping her hand forced her to quicken her pace. Ashes were already falling, not as yet very thickly. I looked round: a dense black cloud was coming up behind us, spreading over the earth like a flood. We had scarcely sat down to rest when darkness fell, not the dark of a moonless or cloudy night, but as if the lamp had been put out in a closed room. You could hear the shrieks of women, the wailing of infants, and the shouting of men....

Check your progress

Some progress
I can identify and alter tenses in words.

Good progress
I can use verb tenses well, and understand the idea of verb moods.

Excellent progress
I can use verb tenses and moods expressively.

3 This account would be even more dramatic in eyewitness style, with the verbs in the *present tense*.

a) Rewrite the passage, changing all the verbs to present tense.

b) Add a subjunctive sentence at the end: 'If we...'

Check your progress

Some progress

- [ ] I can use varied forms of punctuation.
- [ ] I can think about the length and structure of sentences.
- [ ] I can use varied sentence patterns in application.
- [ ] I can write dialogue accurately.
- [ ] I can pick out rhetorical devices in persuasive writing.

Good progress

- [ ] I can use varied forms of punctuation effectively.
- [ ] I can use varied sentence length, order and structure.
- [ ] I can use varied sentence patterns confidently in description.
- [ ] I can write dialogue effectively.
- [ ] I can use rhetorical devices in persuasive writing.

Excellent progress

- [ ] I can use varied punctuation expressively.
- [ ] I can employ varied sentence length, structure and order confidently.
- [ ] I can use varied sentence patterns thoughtfully in description.
- [ ] I can write dialogue imaginatively.
- [ ] I can rhetorical devices forcefully in persuasive writing.

Chapter 6
Select appropriate and effective vocabulary

What's it all about?

In order to write effectively, you need to choose appropriate and striking words to enhance your work and adapt it to your audience and purpose.

This chapter will show you how to

- understand the effects of vocabulary choices
- develop a varied, ambitious vocabulary
- use vocabulary with subtlety and originality
- choose vocabulary that is appropriate to your audience and purpose.

Understand the effects of vocabulary choices

Learning objective

- understand how meaning is affected by the words you choose.

It is important to understand the effects of your vocabulary so that you can make all your ideas clear to the reader.

Getting you thinking

1 With a partner, talk about the difference in tone and **formality** between these two sentences.

> I caught the thief, locked him up and asked him why he'd done it.

> I apprehended the perpetrator, confined him and questioned him as to his motives.

2 Using a dictionary, look up the **etymology** of the following words:

- catch
- thief
- lock
- ask
- do
- apprehend
- perpetrator
- confine
- question
- motive

Glossary

formality: the type of language used – for example, we use formal language when writing to someone we don't know, but informal language when talking to friends

etymology: the origin and changing usage of a word

How does it work?

The first sentence uses words that come from Old English (Anglo-Saxon). The second uses words that came to the language a bit later on, from Norman French. Anglo-Saxon words established physical actions and everyday events, so they often seem quite simple or blunt. Norman French was the language of justice and government after the Norman Conquest of 1066, so they can seem sophisticated and formal.

If you compare the two sentences, you'll notice that the first one (with more Anglo-Saxon words) seems quite everyday and informal, whereas the second sentence (with more Norman French words) sounds more like a formal, written report.

3 Look at the word bank below and decide on the ten words that you think sound more sophisticated and would best fit a formal, written report.

acquaintance	acquire	assault	assistance
documents	first	get	help
hit	incorrect	initial	law
leg	limb	mate	merchandise
papers	rule	stuff	wrong

4 Use a dictionary to check the meanings of the words you have chosen, and then to find out about their etymology. Do they have anything in common?

5 Write a formal account of an incident (such as a robbery at an auction house or someone getting mugged), and include all your chosen words from the word bank above.

Apply your skills

6 Read aloud your formal account to a partner. Highlight the words you have used (other than those from the word bank) that sound particularly formal, serious or official.

7 Discuss with your partner the words you have picked out, and try to come up with alternatives that would sound less formal and sophisticated. For example, if you mention a 'criminal', you could replace it with 'crook' or 'bad guy'.

8 In pairs, try rewriting one of your accounts. This time, instead of it being formal and sophisticated, make it sound informal and everyday – it might even include some humour.

Think about the words that you have discussed, and replace key words and phrases to completely change the tone of the writing.

Check your progress

Some progress
I can select some vocabulary to create a tone.

Good progress
I can choose a range of vocabulary that conveys my chosen tone.

Excellent progress
I can use ambitious vocabulary to establish and sustain different tones.

Develop a varied, ambitious vocabulary

Learning objective
- build up a wider vocabulary.

It is important to develop your vocabulary so that you know a range of ambitious and imaginative words to use in your writing.

Getting you thinking

Look at these two versions of a piece of writing.

> On Sunday, usually a boring day, we went to the fairground. As we walked up the hill I could hear music playing and people calling out happily. Walking over the hill, the fairground was an amazing sight: colourful lights shone and spun while children ran around, screaming with delight or chewing bright pink candyfloss. The smells were just as tempting. The scent of hot dogs drifted up to us, combined with the sweetness of toffee apples and fudge.

> Sundays are usually grey, lifeless and boring. Like a snail slowly heaving itself through thick mud, they seem to drag on interminably. However, last Sunday we went to the fairground. Trudging up Mixley Hill, I began to hear strange, tinny music calling to me, mingled with the happy cries of delighted children. I quickened my pace. The most amazing sight blazed before my eyes: a kaleidoscope of coruscating lights, spinning and merging in all the colours of the rainbow. The panoply of tempting smells was similarly enticing. The thick scent of hot dogs drifted up to us, carrying with it the sweeter aromas of toffee apples and fudge.

 1 Why is the second version better? (Hint: it is not to do with being longer but the way in which things are described.)

How does it work?

Notice the use of

- *metaphor* ('Sundays are usually grey') and *simile* ('like a snail')

- *extra detail*: 'scent' becomes 'thick scent'; 'music' becomes 'strange, tinny music'

- *more descriptive verbs and nouns*: 'drifted', 'trudging', 'blazed', 'kaleidoscope'

- *more complex images* (compare the first sightings of the fairground – the second one is a bit over the top, but so are fairgrounds!)

- *more unusual words*: 'interminably', 'coruscating', 'panoply' (if you don't know what they mean, that's OK – look them up and then use them yourself!)

Now you try it

2 Using a thesaurus and dictionary, find a more ambitious alternative for each of these words:

a) verbs: eat, give, look, stop, think

b) adjectives: dark, dirty, happy, precious, red

3 Think about the different meaning that each of your new words brings with it. Then use your ten new words in an imaginative, entertaining paragraph or two.

> **Top tip**
>
> Every time you come across an unusual word in your reading, look it up and find out what it means. Then remember to use it in your own writing.

Apply your skills

One way to develop your vocabulary is to build up *noun phrases*. Rather than simply using a *noun* (for example, 'There was a *cat*'), add words around it that tell the reader more:

> There was a tired-looking black cat asleep on the stairs.

In this example, the adjectives 'tired-looking' and 'black' have been added to the basic noun 'cat' to make a noun phrase that tells us what the cat looks like. This description has then been extended further by including the state the cat is in (the adjective 'asleep'), and where it is (the preposition 'on', followed by the determiner and noun 'the stairs').

4 Write three paragraphs describing a tropical rainforest. Use a wide range of vocabulary to create imaginative, ambitious descriptions. Try to use all the words in the vocabulary list below.

abundantly	=	in great number (adverb)
effulgent	=	shining brightly (adjective)
emerald	=	green (adjective)
glimmer	=	to shine (verb)
moist	=	a bit wet (adjective)
myriad	=	many (adjective)
tendrils	=	the leafless shoots of a climbing plant (noun)
verdant	=	green with vegetation (adjective)
vertiginous	=	high enough to cause vertigo (adjective)
vividly	=	colourfully (adverb)

Check your progress

Some progress
I can use a range of vocabulary to describe a rainforest effectively.

Good progress
I can use increasingly ambitious vocabulary to create interesting images of a rainforest.

Excellent progress
I can use a range of vocabulary to engage the reader with original, interesting images of a rainforest.

Use vocabulary with subtlety and originality

Learning objective

- make your writing more subtle and original by describing mood and detail.

Writing with subtlety means carefully conveying moods and details. At different times your writing might be elaborate and dramatic or calm and reflective. By choosing your vocabulary carefully, you can make your work that little bit different from everybody else's.

Getting you thinking

Read these two passages.

> This has been a year of strange events: some wonderful, some terrible.
>
> In the autumn a great wind swept through my garden one night, and toppled two oaks, three maples and a chestnut tree, all top-heavy with wet leaves, rooted in sodden earth. Had the gale come a week later the leaves would have been gone and the trees no doubt survived: a week earlier and the earth would have been dry and the roots steadier, and all would have been well. As it was, the chestnut crashed through the conservatory and set off all the alarms, which joined with the sound of the gale to frighten me out of my wits, so that I would have telephoned Carl, my ex-husband, and **forthwith** begged for his forgiveness and the restoration of his protection, but as the chestnut had brought down the wires I couldn't. By the morning the wind had died down and I, Joanna May, was my proper self again, or thought I was.
>
> *The Cloning of Joanna May* by Fay Weldon

Glossary

forthwith: immediately

shrapnel: fragments of a bomb thrown outwards by an explosion

> A volcanic island thrown out of the earth's crust. What was deep is high. What was hidden is visible for all to see. The red peaks of Fyr are a landmark and a warning. No one knows when the island will erupt again, spilling itself in furious melt into the burning sea.
>
> Arum lilies grow here, trumpets blaring light, gunpowder stamens and a flint stalk. The lilies of the field neither toil nor spin but from time to time they explode, strewing the ground with a **shrapnel** of petals; force, fuse, flower.
>
> 'Turn of the World' in *The World and Other Places* by Jeanette Winterson

1 How is the mood of each extract different?

2 What specific words and images are used to create the mood and to help you to picture the scene?

3 In what ways is the first extract more conventional and the second more unusual and metaphorical?

How does it work?

The mood of the first extract is quite reflective. The writer considers what might have happened and there is a lot of uncertainty, which is emphasised through the use of contrasts. The writer also uses everyday references, which make the events seem more commonplace.

The mood created in the second extract is more dramatic, with lots of violent verbs and images of danger. The metaphors create unusual images for the reader. There are also some quite beautiful descriptions that add to this strangeness.

Now you try it

4 Describe someone getting warm by an open fire, and aim to create a calm mood in your writing. Make your descriptions restrained to help produce a peaceful atmosphere. Remember to include some specific nouns.

Apply your skills

5 In pairs, one person should write a description of a house party while the other writes about the state of the house the following morning.

To start with, work together to create a mind-map of the different moods that the two pieces of writing will create. Include details of the vocabulary (including specific nouns) that you could use for each one.

Once you have thought about the moods that you are going to create, work individually to write your descriptions. Take your time to create imaginative and ambitious images. Write for 20 minutes, then share your work with your partner.

Check your progress

Some progress
I can create imaginative descriptions of the house.

Good progress
I can use some subtle vocabulary to convey the house and the mood effectively.

Excellent progress
I can fully convey the house and different moods with subtlety and originality.

Choose vocabulary that is appropriate to your audience and purpose

Learning objective

- engage your reader and achieve your purpose through your selection of vocabulary.

You need to think about who you are writing for (*audience*) and what you are trying to achieve (*purpose*). You should adapt your vocabulary to match your purpose and audience.

Getting you thinking

Look at these two extracts: the first aims to engage and entertain teenagers, while the second informs and entertains older readers about life in Japan.

> Saturday, June the 13th. And Robert Caligari is going to die today. It's a marvellous day. The place is Sandway in Kent, near Lenham, the highest village in the county. It is 7.30 in the morning. It is the sort of day that makes you glad to be alive and it is a Saturday too. To be young on a warm sunny Saturday in June is simply wonderful. And today is the day Robert Caligari is going to die.
>
> *The Boy Who Kicked Pigs* by Tom Baker

> This is clearly one of those districts where it always seems to be Sunday afternoon. Somebody in a house by the corner shop is effortlessly practising Chopin on the piano. A dusty cat rolls in the ruts of the unpaved **streetlet**, yawning in the sunshine. Somebody's aged granny trots off to the supermarket for a litre or two of honourable **sake**. Her iron-grey hair is scraped into so tight a knot in the nape no single hair could ever stray untidily out, and her decent, drab **kimono** is enveloped in the whitest of enormous aprons, trimmed with a sober frill of cotton lace.
>
> *Shaking a Leg* by Angela Carter

Glossary

streetlet: a little street

sake: Japanese rice wine

kimono: a loose, ankle-length garment with wide sleeves, worn in Japan

1 What differences do you notice in the vocabulary of each extract? How does each writer adapt their vocabulary to meet their purpose and audience?

How does it work?

The second extract paints a much more detailed picture for its older readers, and features more specific details and ambitious images. In contrast, the first extract doesn't have as much descriptive detail but uses more immediate (and sometimes shocking) statements to grab the attention of its younger readers.

Now you try it

Read the opening of Ian Fleming's *Casino Royale*, a spy thriller written to entertain older readers.

> The scent and smoke and sweat of a casino are nauseating at three in the morning. Then the soul-erosion produced by high gambling – a compost of greed and fear and nervous tension – becomes unbearable and the senses awake and revolt from it. James Bond suddenly knew that he was tired. He always knew when his body or his mind had had enough and he always acted on the knowledge.
>
> *Casino Royale* by Ian Fleming

2 In pairs, discuss how the extract could be changed to appeal to younger readers (8–10 year olds).

   a) What words or images might need simplifying?

   b) Are there bits you would miss out? Why?

   c) How could you change the structure of the sentences to simplify them?

   d) How would you keep the writing imaginative and entertaining?

Top tip

Look back at the first extract by Tom Baker to get some ideas: simple but effective descriptions, friendly tone, a mixture of long sentences (to describe) and short sentences (to make something clear or to surprise the reader).

Apply your skills

3 Write the opening of a story aimed at younger teenagers. Choose either a romantic comedy about love and relationships or an action-packed adventure story.

Think about the type of story, the kind of vocabulary you will use and how you will make it entertaining.

4 When you have finished your story, swap it with a partner. When they have read it, discuss with them why you chose the vocabulary that you did.

Check your progress

Some progress »
I can usually choose vocabulary to match a genre and an age group.

Good progress »»
I can select effective vocabulary to match a genre and engage an age group.

Excellent progress »»»
I can consistently use varied vocabulary to convey a genre subtly and engage an age group.

Check your progress

Some progress

- [ ] I can select vocabulary to show tone and add specificity.
- [ ] I can use a range of vocabulary effectively.
- [ ] I can use vocabulary to create imaginative descriptions and convey ideas.
- [ ] I can usually choose vocabulary that matches my audience and purpose.
- [ ] I understand where and when some words originate from.

Good progress

- [ ] I can choose a range of vocabulary that matches my meaning.
- [ ] I can use an ambitious range of vocabulary to achieve various effects.
- [ ] I can use descriptive vocabulary with some subtlety and originality.
- [ ] I can select effective vocabulary that matches my audience and purpose.
- [ ] I can use words from different times and places to change my meaning.

Excellent progress

- [ ] I can use ambitious vocabulary to create specific effects and make my meaning clear.
- [ ] I can consistently use an ambitious range of vocabulary to achieve a very successful range of effects.
- [ ] I can consistently use descriptive vocabulary to convey complex and thoughtful ideas with subtlety and originality.
- [ ] I can consistently match my ambitious, effective vocabulary to my audience and purpose.
- [ ] I can explore how words from different times and places can bring different tone and meaning to my writing.

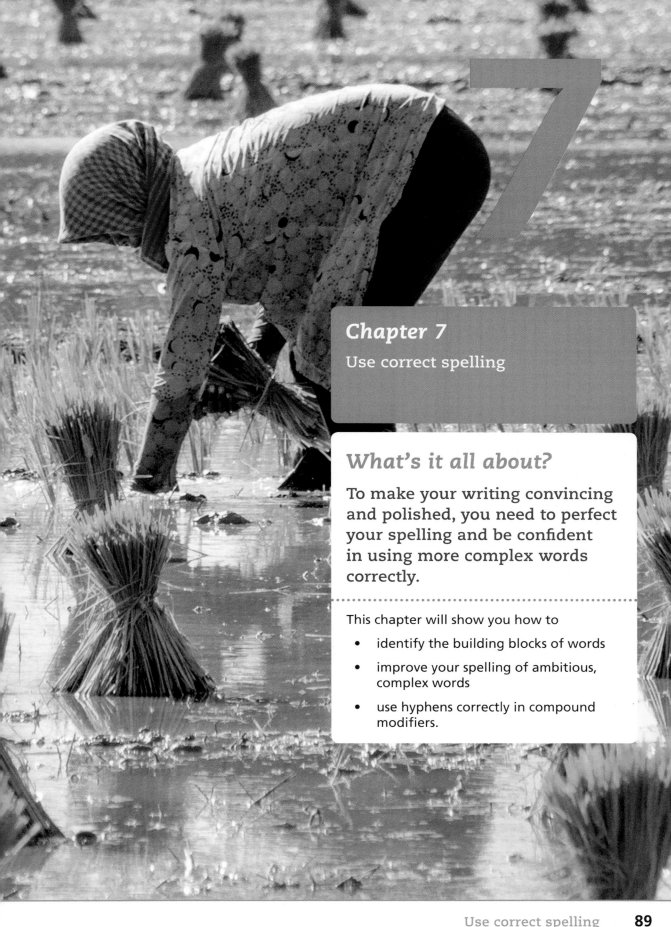

Chapter 7

Use correct spelling

What's it all about?

To make your writing convincing and polished, you need to perfect your spelling and be confident in using more complex words correctly.

This chapter will show you how to

- identify the building blocks of words
- improve your spelling of ambitious, complex words
- use hyphens correctly in compound modifiers.

Identify the building blocks of words

Learning objective

- spell more complex words by visualising them.

As words become more complex, they often don't follow simple spelling rules.

Getting you thinking

It can help to visualise the *building blocks* of words when trying to remember a spelling. This doesn't mean spelling words phonetically (by the way they sound). Instead, try to picture how the different syllables are spelled and then put them together.

1. Choose any five words of two or more syllables, and break them up into their different syllable blocks.

How does it work?

Notice that different words contain similar syllable blocks. So the 'bull' sound in words like 'laughable' is usually spelled 'ble', while the 'shun' sound in words like 'attention' is usually spelled 'tion'.

If you get used to recognising and visualising these different blocks, this should help you with your spelling.

Now you try it

2. Break the following words into their syllable blocks:

   invest, person, rebel

   Then see how you can alter the blocks to build similar words. For example, 'possible':

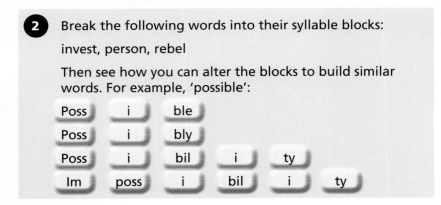

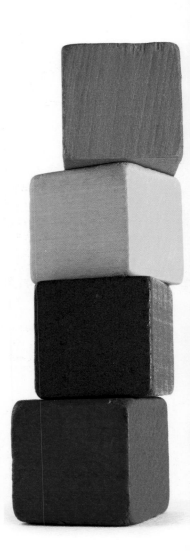

3 Choose three more words of your own to break into blocks and build new words from. Do any of your blocks contain similar spellings?

Apply your skills

4 Make a list of words that start with the following syllable blocks:

at el head mag tel

For example:

attitude   electric   headstrong   magnify   telescope

5 Make a list of words that end with the following syllable blocks:

tion ious ity our age

For example:

sensation   envious   enormity   harbour   baggage

6 As an extension, play a spelling game with your partner. Take it in turns to pick a word of more than two syllables and challenge your partner to spell it. Write out the number of letters as dashes, as if you were playing hangman. So, for example, 'xylophone':

_ _ _ _ _ _ _ _ _

If your partner gets it right straight away, they score five points. If not, they can keep swapping a point for a letter to help them. For example:

_ _ _ _ P _ _ _ _

See who manages to score the most points!

If you don't know a word, try to break it down into syllable blocks and visualise the spelling.

Top tip

The more times you see a word, the easier it is to visualise it – so it's a good idea to increase the amount of reading that you do at home. Whether you read novels, comics or magazines, they're full of spellings that your brain will start to remember!

Check your progress

Some progress

I can spell the start and end of some complex words correctly.

Good progress

I can identify syllable blocks to help me spell most complex words correctly.

Excellent progress

My spelling is excellent when using complex vocabulary.

Improve your spelling of ambitious, complex words

Learning objective

- improve your spelling of more complex words.

When you start to use more ambitious, complex vocabulary in your writing, you probably won't know all the spellings. Some words you will have found in a thesaurus, but others you may just have remembered from books or heard people use.

Getting you thinking

1 In pairs, pick one column of words each. Spend two minutes trying to memorise these spellings (you might know some already). Then test each other. Which words were the hardest? Did you find any special way to help you memorise them?

accommodate	buccaneer
guillotine	equilibrium
loquacious	onomatopoeia
somnolent	separate
tyrannical	voracious

> **Top tip**
>
> Get used to using a dictionary to check words. Also, make up your own rules and reminders to help you spell complex words.

How does it work?

You may have learned the spellings by visualising syllable blocks (such as som + no + lent), or by using a memorable phrase (for example, 'there is a rat in separate'). With a word like 'onomatopoeia', it looks really hard but is actually easy until the end; so, rather than worrying about the on + o + mat + o part, you could simply learn the unusual 'poeia'.

Now you try it

From the remote, mist-shrouded mountins of the north, to the rich and fertile lowlands of the Mekong Delta, Vietnam is horntingly beautiful. Patchworks of briliant green rice paddies fade into the mountinus horrizon and reach down to the sweeping, desserted beaches caracteristic of the drammatic coasteline. Set in this seenically stunning land, the historic towns and sleepy fishing villages incapsculate the bygone charm of Asia's past. Friendly and incredibly hospittable locals invite you into their homes to sip tea and chat about life in their fasinating land. These chance incounters will leave lasting memmories that will forever tempte you to return.

2 Correct the spelling mistakes in this piece of travel writing. Use a dictionary to help you, and think about the different ways in which you could learn any new spellings that you find.

Afterwards, challenge your partner to spell some of the words.

Apply your skills

3 Use a dictionary and a thesaurus to help you complete this crossword. Each clue gives you the first letter and definition of the word. As you work, try to remember what the words mean and how they are spelled.

ACROSS
8   E. To put out (a fire).
10   L. Extremely comfortable.
12   J. Person whose job is to make decisions in a law court.
13   C. To consider something.
19   M. Concerned with money and self-gain.
22   X. A plant able to grow in very dry conditions.
24   Y. A light sailing vessel.
25   I. New.
26   P. A ghost.

DOWN
1   S. At the same time.
2   N. A feeling of sickness.
3   R. Pains in the joints and muscles.
4   G. To shine, especially when wet.
5   K. Information gained from experience.
6   T. Irregular or disturbed.
7   O. To confuse or bewilder.
9   W. Twist as if in pain.
11   D. How deep something is.
14   A. Fake or man-made.
15   B. Polished.
16   U. Requiring immediate action.
17   V. Poisonous.
18   H. Clean.
20   F. From another country.
21   Z. Enthusiasm and hard work.
23   Q. Nicely old-fashioned.

Check your progress

Some progress
I can spell common words correctly, including some that are often misspelt.

Good progress
I can spell most words, including some complex vocabulary.

Excellent progress
My spelling is excellent when using complex, ambitious vocabulary.

Use hyphens correctly in compound modifiers

Learning objective

- improve your use of hyphens.

You already know that some prefixes need hyphens, but hyphens should also be used to make the meaning clear when adjectives are joined together to create *descriptive compounds*.

Getting you thinking

 1 Read these sentences and, in pairs, discuss how the hyphen affects the meaning in each case.

a) He was a little-respected politician.

b) An American-football player visited our school.

c) It was a tired-looking house.

How does it work?

If you have two words that jointly modify a word (a *compound modifier*), the words need to be hyphenated to keep the meaning clear. A 'little respected politician' (no hyphen) would be someone who was small and respected, rather than someone who people had no respect for ('little-respected politician').

However, if the compound modifier comes *after* the word that it affects, there is no need to use a hyphen. For example, 'That politician is little respected.'

If the words aren't modifying anything, they don't need to be hyphenated. So 'an *American-football* player' needs a hyphen because it tells us what sport the person plays, but 'They were playing *American football*' doesn't need a hyphen because 'American football' is just being used as a noun here.

You also don't need to use a hyphen if the modifying words contain an *adverb* (for example, 'It was a thinly veiled threat'), unless the meaning would be unclear without the hyphen.

> **Top tip**
>
> Don't confuse a hyphen and a dash. A hyphen is used to join two words (or a word and a prefix) together, and a dash is a longer punctuation mark. Dashes can be used in pairs to do the job of two commas or brackets. For example: 'The cats – of which she had seventeen – were crawling all over the house.' Unlike the hyphen, there are spaces around each dash.

Now you try it

 2 Copy out the five sentences below, and add a hyphen where you think it is appropriate.

a) She bought a buried metal detector.

b) The song was well rehearsed by the class.

c) We need a short term plan.

d) He was a first rate doctor.

e) They own a high speed boat.

3 Copy out these five sentences, and remove any incorrect hyphens. When you have finished correcting the ten sentences share your work with a partner and explain why you made your changes.

a) She was barely-visible in the darkness.

b) The teacher was well-respected.

c) I am going to Northern-Ireland.

d) The highly-rated film made lots of money.

e) The food in the restaurant was under-cooked.

> **Top tip**
>
> If you use two or more adjectives that don't act as a compound modifier, remember to separate them using a comma or 'and'. For example: 'The bus was small, red and shiny.'

Apply your skills

4 Working with a partner, and using a dictionary and thesaurus to help you, make a list of hyphenated compound modifiers. Use the four affixes below to start you off. You can then add any other words you can think of.

Affix	Example
well-	well-bred
little-	little-known
-flavoured	orange-flavoured
-minded	absent-minded

5 Using the list that you have made, write a paragraph containing lots of compound modifiers. Remember that you only use the hyphen if the compound comes before the word it's modifying.

6 Can you make any silly phrases by deliberately making a mistake with the hyphen in some compound modifiers? This will show that you can understand the importance of the hyphen in making your meaning clear. For example: 'I was a horse riding champion when I was younger.'

Check your progress

Some progress

I can use hyphens accurately to create some compound modifiers.

Good progress

I usually use hyphens accurately when forming a range of compound modifiers.

Excellent progress

I use hyphens accurately when forming an ambitious range of compound modifiers.

Check your progress

Some progress

- ☐ I can use hyphens accurately to create some compound modifiers.
- ☐ I can spell common words and most homophones correctly.
- ☐ I can use prefixes and suffixes correctly.

Good progress

- ☐ I usually use hyphens accurately when forming a range of compound modifiers.
- ☐ I can spell most words, including some complex vocabulary.
- ☐ I can identify syllable blocks to help me spell complex words correctly.

Excellent progress

- ☐ I use hyphens accurately when forming an ambitious range of compound modifiers.
- ☐ My spelling is excellent, including complex, ambitious vocabulary.

Teacher Guide

The general aim of these books is the practical and everyday application of **Assessment for Learning**: to ensure every child knows how they are doing and what they need to do to improve. The specific aim is to help every child progress and for you to be able to track that progress.

The books empower the student by modelling the essential skills needed, and by allowing them to practise and then demonstrate independently what they know and can do across every reading and writing strand. They help the teacher by providing opportunities to gather and review secure evidence of day-to-day progress in each strand. Where appropriate (and especially at lower levels) the books facilitate teacher scaffolding of such learning and assessment.

The series offers exercises and examples that we hope will not only help students add descriptive power and nuance to their vocabulary but also expand the grammatical constructions they can access and use: above all, the ability to write and read in sentences (paragraphs, texts) – to think consciously in complete thoughts. We aim at fuller, more complex self-expression – developing students' ability to express themselves simply or with complexity and the sense to choose when each mode of expression is apt.

Each chapter progresses through a series of emphases, to be practised and mastered before bringing it back to the real reading and writing (of whole texts) in which all these – suitably polished – skills can be applied.

The *Aiming for...* series has been extremely popular in schools. This new edition retains all that was successful about the old but has improved it further in several significant ways.

- This book positively tracks progress in the new curriculum, so each chapter has been updated to ensure thorough coverage of the Key Stage 3 Programme of Study and the Grammar, Vocabulary and Punctuation Appendix to the Key Stage 2 Programme of Study.

- The new progress categories of Some/Good/Excellent correspond to the old sublevels of low Level 6, secure Level 6 and high Level 6.

- A matching chart to the new curriculum is available on www.collins. co.uk/ aimingfor.

- The 'Applying your skills' section of each topic is now consistently focused on longer writing tasks designed to build the writing stamina and independence needed for GCSE.

Gareth Calway and Mike Gould
Series Editors

1 Write with a clear emphasis on narration rather than plot

How does it work?
Chandler explained his *noir* world in *The Simple Art of Murder*:

But down these mean streets a man must go who is not himself mean, who is neither tarnished nor afraid...The detective...is the hero... He must be...a man of honor – by instinct...without thought of it, and certainly without saying it. He must be the best man in his world.

Chandler's detective-narrator talks to you in world-weary poetry: '[Kingsley] was about six feet two and not much of it soft.' The sentences have a rhythm, a repeated pattern like music. The adjectives, noun phrases and descriptive verbs are strong, like the character they describe.

Now you try it
Remind students that plot is just what *happens*.

The middle paragraph is made up of four *statement sentences* to *describe* Kingsley. The sentences have a strong *beat*, a *pattern* like music: 'He was...', 'His eyes...', 'He filled...', 'His manner...' The *adjectives*, *noun phrases* and *descriptive verbs* are strong, like him, and in a *repeated* pattern: 'stone grey...cold light', 'smooth grey flannel...narrow chalk stripe', 'filled a large size...and filled it elegantly'.

One metaphor in the second extract is 'minutes went by on tiptoe', and the overall tone is wry – as in 'helped them laugh'. The sentence patterns convey toughness.

Apply your skills
In pairs, students can read out their descriptions and then redraft them based on what they thought worked best/didn't work. Compare their description of Miss Fromsett's eyes with Chandler's – 'large dark eyes that looked like they might warm up at the right time and in the right place'.

2 Write in character sustaining a role or voice

Begin by explaining that in non-fiction writing this would be 'adopt a viewpoint that isn't necessarily your own'.

How does it work?
Thomo's speech is written with the following features:

- chippy exclamation ('Watchit!')

- spirited rhetorical questions ('I have to fight back, don't I? Why should they pick on me?')

- upbeat tone (throughout the extract)

- direct simple statements ('They call me Thomo' and 'Can't resist a fight')

- repetition for emphasis and an upbeat rhythm ('Why should they pick on me? Why should they pick on me just 'cause I'm small?')

- informal language or colloquialisms ("cause', 'see red').

Explain that a *rhetorical question* is really a statement.

Draw out in discussion with students that all of these features come from first *imagining you are Thomo* and then *writing the way he would speak*. They won't be able to write in his voice unless they first think like him and imagine they are him.

Point out that much fiction writing is narrated in a voice and point of view that is not the author's.

Now you try it
Allow the students to work in pairs and discuss why they feel things have changed for the headmaster. Has society changed? Or is the headmaster losing his grip?

Apply your skills

Remind them that Lana will speak as freely as she does in the monologue because the social worker 'understands, listens'. But the social worker is still doing a job and Lana is still a troubled teenager.

3 Choose an effective narrative style

Getting you thinking

Ask students in pairs to focus on *how* the narrator tells the story. Would they have done it in a different way?

How does it work?

The narrative sounds adult, detached: a man looking back at childhood, not a child speaking. Consider the complicating effect of the compound *modal forms* ('whether I shall…' and 'whether that station will be') and the imperative modal 'these pages must show', which makes it sound as if the pages are separate from the man writing them. The narrator uses *formal language* and *long complex sentences* to address (rather than chat to) his reader: 'I record', 'I have been informed', 'it was remarked', 'simultaneously'. It is a bookish language and style.

Now you try it

The cheery informality of Huck, including the 'bad' grammar, is engaging – as if a child has taken over a grown-up's job. Later spelling mistakes – for example, 'sivilised' – will create the same mood of subversion.

The narrator is a character in both these *bildungsromans*. Dickens wrote 'No-one can ever believe this Narrative…more than I have believed it in the writing' (preface to *David Copperfield*, London, October 1850). *The Catcher in the Rye*, J.D. Salinger's *bildungsroman* of a troubled late 1940s New York teenager called Holden Caulfield, is said to voice teenage angst more than any other.

Apply your skills

Point out to students that many fiction authors mix together real and imagined events to create their stories – the students may decide to do the same in their own writing.

4 Write using a range of stylistic devices to create effects

How does it work?

Explain to students that *onomatopoeia* is the term that describes words or phrases that *sound* like what they describe.

Rhythm is another effect that creates the sounds of a poem. The rhythm of this poem is *iambic pentameter*, but 'Bare black cliff clang'd' puts four *stresses* together. This unexpected change of rhythm *imitates* the hammering sound heard by the knight.

The *setting* also suggests the knight's cold, lonely mood, and therefore acts as a *metaphor* for the knight's feelings.

Repetition – of *sounds* (and *images* of ice and dark and cold) – gives *emphasis* and helps readers hear/see the loneliness.

Longer lines, like the last two lines of this poem, can have a more thoughtful, spacious feeling than shorter ones. *Short lines*, like short sentences, often convey tension, excitement or finality. However, in this poem the sentence of long lines leading up to the dash does not feel spacious or leisurely because it is packed with action, sound effects and pictures. Remind students that it is always good to cut out 'padding' in the way that line-writing encourages, even if they're not writing in verse.

Now you try it

Point out to students that poetry is part word-music, based on *sound* (as in the comic-strip panels), but remind them that the words chosen must also have a suitable *meaning*.

Apply your skills
Students should decide whether their lines will be long, short, end-stopped or open. Explain that *end-stopped* means that punctuation (especially a full stop) 'stops' the end of the line; open (or *enjambment*) means that the line end has no punctuation and the sentence continues through it.

5 Choose effective vocabulary for your purpose

How does it work?
Explain to students that the word 'Childe' in the title tells us that this poem is about a knight, and point out that the verse contains lots of otherworldly and old-fashioned words that conjure up a faraway, long-ago world. However, the poem begins – startlingly – in the middle of an unexplained conversation, and after that Browning keeps us guessing as to what is going on at least until the third verse. All we have is a spooky meeting in a deserted road with a menacing figure.

The form used is both suspense and quest narrative. There are twelve lines of suspense before the 'reveal' of the word 'if', and the poem's vocabulary indicates that it is also a quest narrative. A description of a man asking his way to the post office would not use such convoluted sentences ('…with malicious eye…and mouth…') and so many otherworldly nouns (Dark Tower, knight) and adjectives (hoary, ominous).

Now you try it
The correct order is: path, comes, glooms, bath, wrath, spumes.

Apply your skills
Students may want to find out more about the wasteland in Browning's poem, or they could use others that they are familiar with (such as Frodo's quest across Mordor to Mount Doom). They could also invent their own wasteland.

Tell students that the rest of Browning's poem includes the following 'nightmare' features, to give them some ideas of what this wasteland constitutes:

- bats
- a skeletal horse
- funeral banners
- weeds
- a black serpent-like stream
- thistles
- grass 'scant as hair in leprosy'
- toads in a poisoned tank
- bog, clay and rubble
- a huge black bird
- the noise of many bells
- a 'squat tower'.

The Dark Tower itself is unexpectedly – and therefore imaginatively – dull and ordinary. This shows how evil often has an 'ordinary' face.

6 Write reflectively and analytically to explore issues or ideas

How does it work?
Help students identify exaggeration and generalisation in the text. In the apology, there is also some light-hearted and conversational language to win over the reader. Establish that the modals do soften, but the writer of the post also sticks to his guns. After the polite qualifications he still gives a confident command – if you can't accept what I say on these terms, delete me.

Now you try it
The writer's viewpoint is that it is refreshing to see women presented as winners rather than as catty rivals. Exaggerations (to entertain and thus win over) include pouting Leah's mouth

falling off; generalisations include 'the female front bickering' and supporting anecdotes include Karren Brady 'looking despairingly at the sisterhood'. The prominent 'Don't get me wrong' and 'But on the plus side' act as softeners against the critical edge of the writing.

Apply your skills
Make the point that many social media interactions seek to provoke – threads often start with reaction-seeking assertions. Ask students what kinds of analytical or reflective passage they might want to write that would be better for using softer language.

Chapter 2   Produce texts that are appropriate to task, reader and purpose

1 Write creatively for specific effects

Getting you thinking
Read the poem aloud to students to emphasise the short, staccato sound of the lines. Then ask students to work in pairs, re-reading the poem aloud before discussing the questions. You could introduce the idea of *conventions* at this point – for example, by eliciting the idea that the endings of poems often resolve or rewrite what has gone before.

How does it work?
The key idea here is to elicit how *form and content combine to match purpose*. Concept check this by asking how the effect would change if the poem was to begin like this:

> 'The shadows of the café sign cast a pale light,
>
> An emptiness illuminated by my lateness, and her flight…'

We would get the sense that this was an adult's perception of love, for a start, and we might also perceive it to be less modern in setting and tone.

Now you try it
Read the second poem aloud once or twice. After the first two pairs activities, take feedback

on the discussion points. The 'sound-events' the students might locate are: the 'slushy sand'; the 'tap at the pane'; the 'quick sharp scratch'; and perhaps the 'voice less loud' and the 'two hearts beating'. Elicit the idea that the narrator doesn't 'appear' until the fifth line – unlike in the first poem – and that we learn next to nothing about his lover.

When students have completed the grid, compile a class grid on the board and talk about the effect or tone created by each feature in both poems. For example, the first person 'I' makes both poems focus predominantly on the narrator's experience. The comparison could be started as a piece of shared writing on the board.

Apply your skills
Once students have had a chance to consider the sort of poem they want to write, go round the class and ask them to explain what they have decided to do. Question them about 'tone' to gauge if they are able to match form to desired outcome. Make sure they spend time creating their palette of good phrases or lines. You might wish to display final poems, and ask students to look at these and make notes on the tone and effect created in each case.

2 Use a range of techniques to match your genre and purpose

Getting you thinking
When the students have had a chance to individually write their lists, ask for feedback and compile a class list. You might wish to add to the list with ideas such as: vivid detail

about buildings or landscape; short anecdotes about meetings or funny/frightening moments; references to local customs, clothing, food and so on; journeys/modes of transport; communication issues, and so on.

Read the text together as a class, and check the class list against the text to see how well Tim Nollen's travel writing does the job.

How does it work?

Talk through the list here, and ask students to explain each point or identify further examples. In particular, focus on how the writer matches sudden action (arrival or loss of valuables) with shorter or minor sentences – 'This was it!' and 'Impossible!' – and how these reflect the narrator's swings in mood and behaviour.

Now you try it

Make clear to students that their account doesn't have to be based on a real occurrence. If they are struggling for ideas, suggest they look at recent news reports of events overseas or at images of destinations abroad.

Ensure it is clear that one of the conventions they are trying to imitate is the way the text develops – journey, arrival/relief, panic – and that their choices of sentences should match the arc of the story.

Apply your skills

Students could look at a grid listing Tim Nollen's travel writing skills while they write their draft, and tick off the different techniques as they use them in their own text.

3 Write persuasively for a particular audience

Getting you thinking

Check students are clear what the word 'convention' means before they read the speech – namely, an accepted or common feature or pattern that we associate with a specific form of writing. Remind students that speeches usually

- develop and maintain a clear viewpoint
- use rhetorical techniques to emphasise the important points
- make calculated appeals to their audience (or audiences).

If possible, show students video footage of the Obama speech before they read it: the speech can easily be found on YouTube. Ask them what they notice about the way the speech is delivered and the audience's reaction to it.

How does it work?

Barack Obama is making this speech to celebrate his victory in the election race, to thank all those who have helped in the election campaign, and to set out his vision for the USA.

He tries to appeal to a wide audience by making reference to people of all races, religions and ages, to make them feel involved in his success. He stresses that his victory was achieved through the efforts of ordinary American people.

He also acknowledges the historic nature of being elected as the first black president of the United States. Although his speech is deliberately inclusive, he makes subtle references to the civil rights movement that laid the foundations for this social change, borrowing the lyrics from Sam Cooke's song 'A Change Gonna Come', which was an anthem for the civil rights movement in the 1960s ('It's been a long time coming, but I know a change gonna come'). This song was inspired in part by an incident in 1963 when Cooke and his band tried to register at a 'whites only' motel in Louisiana and were arrested for supposedly disturbing the peace.

Students might be interested to learn that Obama uses several classical rhetorical techniques, known by their Greek names as

- *anaphora*: the repetition of a phrase at the start of a series of sentences ('It's the answer told by lines that stretched…It's the answer spoken by young and old…')
- *tricolon*: the division of a sentence into a series of three ('If there is anyone out there who still doubts…who still wonders…who still questions…')
- *epiphora*: the repetition of a word or phrase at the end of a series of sentences ('tonight is your answer…This is your victory').

Apply your skills

Encourage students to think about what the practical implications for the school would be if the day started later: arranging school buses, cleaning and managing the school, organising staff working hours, and so on.

It might be fun for at least some members of the class to perform their speeches. The rest of the class could take on the roles of the audience (the senior management team, three governors and the parents of some Year 11 students).

Extension

You could ask more able students to do the following tasks.

Draw up some tough questions to ask journalist Gill Hornby about her views. See if you can successfully find holes in her argument. Role-play the conversation.

Draft a letter in response to Gill Hornby's article/ Dr Kelly's intentions, giving your opinion on the issue of a late start to the school day.

4 Adapt what you have read for different purposes

Getting you thinking

Allow students to work in pairs.

How does it work?

One text is a part of a children's adventure novel (*Skeleton Key* by Anthony Horowitz) and the other is from a newspaper article. Each text will have been written with certain conventions in mind, and they would use different conventions if they were rewritten in another form.

Now you try it

Allow students to jot down answers to the questions.

Students might think about how the kangaroo got into the suburb, and about why it then decided to enter the house. They might add dialogue between Mr and Mrs Ettlin and their children, or focus on their thoughts and feelings as the injured kangaroo rampages through their home. The struggle between Mr Ettlin and the kangaroo could be told through the eyes of a witness, perhaps the son.

Students might leave out some information concerning where the Ettlins live.

They might also speed up the fight between Mr Ettlin and the kangaroo, and use short sentences to describe the struggle and to keep the action exciting.

Students could reasonably use any viewpoint except Leighton's, as he doesn't witness the first part of the action. Alternatively, they could use a narrator's viewpoint. Some students might choose to write about the events from the point of view of the kangaroo.

Apply your skills

First, ask students to decide what information would go where in the report. You might draw an 'inverted pyramid' on the board and get students to complete it. For example:

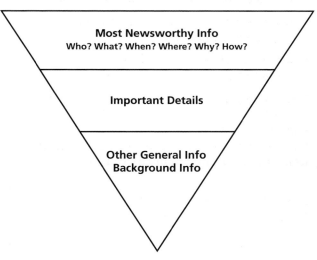

They can then draft the report, building in extra details (such as direct quotes).

5 Adapt the formality of your writing to match the purpose and task

Getting you thinking

The short interview could be read aloud in pairs, or you could ask two confident students to perform/read it to the whole class. Then, ask for suggestions for Questions 1 and 2. Possible responses might be:

- Use synonyms for words that are repeated ('culling', 'killing') and cut text in places to avoid repetition of ideas/points.

- Take out speech 'fillers' such as 'well', and informal words/phrases such as 'stacks', 'gonna' and so on.

- Change references to personal pronouns such as 'you' and 'we'.

How does it work?

You may need to go over the conventions of reported speech, and draw attention to the role of 'that' as a conjunction with the past tense form to introduce the relative clause. To concept check this, you could give students two or three other examples of direct speech to turn into reported speech. For example:

'I believe in free speech,' said Jo = 'Jo said that she believed in free speech.'

'I hate people who keep pet snakes,' said Ryan. = 'Ryan said that he hated people who kept pet snakes.'

Now you try it

Once students have completed their own versions, ask them to swap their work with a partner. They should then check whether they have successfully turned their own work into a more formal piece of writing, and whether

they were able to include one example of direct quotation. Here is one possible model:

> An anonymous protester argued that the proposed badger cull was not going to prevent TB. He also asserted that extensive research had been done and that there is 'no hard evidence' to justify a cull, according to scientists. He went on to add that only 6% of badgers had TB, so any action would have a limited effect. In addition, he argued that it was the movement of cattle around the country that was to blame for its spread. However, the question of why the government and DEFRA are so convinced the cull is right remains unanswered.

Apply your skills

Students should read the text individually and jot down their answers to the questions. Check what they have noted down, as they will need to get this right before writing it up. For example:

Key points made:

- Protesters don't have to cope with the loss of their livestock, as happened this winter.

- The farmer's livestock is reared on his own farm and slaughtered locally, so the animals are not transported around the UK.

- The farmer does everything in the recommended, legal and official way.

For writing up the next part of the article, remind the students to keep their tenses consistent and to embed any quotations fluently. For example:

'Alan Rickway, a local farmer, said, 'We've got to do something!'

1 Effectively control and sequence your work, thinking about the reader's reaction

Getting you thinking
Explain to students that the play is about a homeless teenager called Link, and how he survives in London, and a psychopath called Shelter, who devises an evil scheme to get the homeless off the streets for ever.

How does it work?
The characters' lines should be written in the *tenses*, *accent*, *formality*, *voice* and *tone* that they would actually use. Draw out from students that the playwright has juxtaposed these two scenes so that we see Link first and identify with his situation, making the shift to Shelter all the more shocking.

The audience's reaction is controlled by stage directions, sequencing of scenes, and the language that each character uses.

We are encouraged to feel sympathy for Link. This is immediately shown by the fact that

- he is dirty, hungry, bored and homeless
- people just ignore him, and one person drops a crisp packet at his feet
- he talks to us directly, first taking a good look at the audience as if wary.

In contrast, Shelter is presented as an unpleasant character from the start:

- he sniggers at the sinister word 'executed'
- his soup dribbles from his mouth as he speaks
- his rude 'Get. Lost.' is made ruder by the one-word sentences
- the thick curtains suggest deception; his comfortable surroundings contrast with Link's.

Apply your skills
When students are redrafting their work in Activity 10, explain that their final edit will come later and will include proofreading.

2 Summarise and organise material from different sources

Getting you thinking
In Activity 2 about the 'Bob the Cat' article, ask students if they spotted 'homeless for more than a decade' and 'people who were facing difficult times'. The central story about 'stray, injured Bob' and the book he inspired is not about homeless people in general, although their plight provides the sad background to the happier story – which is 'the exception that proves the rule'.

How does it work?
Explain to students that a summary is as much about what they leave out as what they put in – omitting not only unnecessary words but also irrelevant ideas. On the other hand, it is vital to include all that is relevant, though in a condensed form.

Apply your skills
Emphasise to the students that they have already found and summarised the relevant information, which overwhelmingly proves the MP to be wrong. It is now a matter of organising this information for the purpose of the article, to show how serious the growing problem of youth homelessness is.

3 Use a range of features to signal the text's direction to the reader

Getting you thinking
Students should read the speech with care. They might like to read it through silently several times and then practise reading it aloud, in pairs or in small groups.

Now you try it
Remind students while they are planning their speeches that they need to perform the speech well to maximise the effect of their words. Ask them to make a note of the following points:

- They should speak clearly and loudly.

- It is important that they speak at their normal pace – not too quickly or too slowly.

- They should vary the tone of their voice and avoid hesitations.

- It is important that they keep eye contact with the audience.

- They should think about their body language

– it is better to stand up straight and appear confident.

- Finally, it is a good idea for them to use hand gestures to emphasise points – but only now and again.

Apply your skills
As students listen to the speeches, they should take notes on how each speaker has dealt with the different features that have been discussed:

- structure – was it well organised, with a strong start and finish? How could it be improved?

- content – was the talk interesting? Why did the talk persuade you to vote for that person? Or dissuade you?

- volume and clarity – did the speaker vary their tone of voice? Did the speech have a good pace? Did the speaker look at and engage with the audience?

4 Develop clear and effective introductions

How does it work?
The first two one-sentence paragraphs emphasise how afraid the narrator is, and why, but say nothing of who the narrator is and what they are afraid of. The third paragraph adds that the narrator thinks someone may be coming, and later paragraphs add place names and sightings of smoke.

Now you try it
Explain to students that different texts require different openings. A story, a speech, a web page and a letter begin very differently, as their purposes are usually different. They all need to grab the reader's attention, but where a story might reveal key information slowly –

this being part of its pleasure for the reader – an information web page needs to involve the reader instantly before they click on to a different page.

Apply your skills
Ask students to think about what information they want the reader to know at the start of the story. They shouldn't give them too much information, as it will spoil any surprises later on. They may choose, for instance, to delay telling the reader who the narrator is and why they are alone. They should play around with the structure of their work – they could use short paragraphs, as in the extract from *Z for Zachariah*.

5 Manage information, ideas and events to maximise the effect on the reader

Ask students to bring in a range of tabloid and broadsheet newspapers for this lesson.

Getting you thinking
Emphasise that a 'broadsheet' or 'quality' newspaper is not necessarily better than a tabloid but serves a different readership and purpose. However 'brash' *The Sun* is by broadsheet standards, it successfully uses all the devices listed in the bullet points to analyse a new trend (selfies) and its psychological dangers in six punchy paragraphs.

Now you try it
Draw out that the more leisurely stylistic features of the broadsheet – longer sentences and paragraphs, thoughtful pictures, a more studious (less 'vulgar', if you like) engagement with readers – explore Malala's individual personality. While the first article limits itself to a surface look at Emma Power's identity (a 'selfie addict'), the second article gives a more *detailed* analysis of its subject.

Apply your skills
The students are aiming their article at readers of a similar age, so they should remember to use language and presentational devices that will keep their audience interested. A tabloid article really grabs the reader's attention, with lots of information packed into carefully chosen words. An article with broadsheet features might suit student readers who will take the time to thoughtfully consider an issue. Both approaches involve the use of different, but equally important, writing skills.

An interesting slant would be to take one of the issues and make it controversial.

For example:

Unfit Sports Hall

Money wasted on sub-standard sports hall

Chapter 4   **Construct paragraphs and use cohesion**

1 Structure a fiction paragraph for effect

Getting you thinking
Students should quickly pick up that

- Isa Whitney was addicted to opium

- he became a slave to the drug

- friends and relatives pitied him

- opium changed the way he looked.

Apply your skills
Allow students to work in pairs to create a bullet-point list of ideas before they start writing.

If students run out of ideas, they could use the following:

- The surprise could be that the person they are describing is in terrible danger for some reason.

- The person described could be someone who used to be very successful but has now fallen upon hard times.

- There could be flashbacks to incidents in the character's earlier life that hint at how they have come to be in their current situation.

Finally, develop the idea into a full short story.

2 Decide how and where to start a new paragraph

How does it work?
Ask students: are there any sentences in the extract that they could move around to create a better cohesion between paragraphs?

Now you try it
Explain that in a dramatic monologue, splitting the text into cohesive paragraphs can help to create pauses and focus the audience's attention.

Here, the skill will be not just to create new paragraphs but also to isolate specific sentences for effect.

Apply your skills
When students are redrafting their monologue, advise them that they can further develop the unity of theme in their paragraphs by asking themselves the following questions:

- Do the sentences that are not related to the central theme of their paragraph contain vital information? (If the answer is no, they should cut out these sentences.)

- If the sentences *do* contain vital information, could they be moved into existing paragraphs? Or could the students create a further paragraph containing these sentences?

3 Create cohesion in non-fiction

Getting you thinking
The purpose of linking the paragraphs is to show a clear theme running through the entire piece, ensuring that the writing flows well and displays a clear, sustained logic.

- Paragraph One: This ends with the fact that teams cannot do well without a brilliant manager.

- Paragraph Two: Brian Clough is introduced as an example of a brilliant manager.

- Paragraphs Three and Four: We learn what Clough's teams achieved.

- Paragraph Five: We discover how Clough motivated his teams. This links up with the first paragraph, which informed us that teams cannot achieve great things without a brilliant manager.

How does it work?
What other cohesive devices can students find in the extract?

Other useful connectives include: first(ly), second(ly), third(ly), next, after, similarly, likewise, as with, like, compared with, otherwise, unlike on the other hand, in contrast.

Now you try it
Get students to work in pairs. Set a time limit, and when the time is up ask some pairs to report back and discuss the reasons for their changes. Invite discussion of different opinions.

Apply your skills
Get students to bullet-point their ideas and show their plans to a partner before they start writing.

When the students have finished their pieces, ask them to re-read their own writing from the point of view of their intended audience. Who are their readers?

Explain to students that it may help them to leave their writing for a day or two before re-reading it, so that they have a fresher perspective. They can then redraft their writing, editing out bits they feel do not work.

4 Write cohesively for a purpose

How does it work?
Longer, more complex sentence hold all the separate parts of a thought together in proper order around the *main idea*. For instance, the main idea of the second paragraph is that bees do a 'waggle dance', and the *supporting information* – the purpose of this waggle dance – is included as a *subordinate clause*. The writer uses a comma and the word 'which' to connect this subordinate clause to the rest of the sentence.

Highlight another example of connective writing for the students:

In the first sentence of the third paragraph, the writer uses an extended compound adverb and adjectival noun phrase – 'beat its wings rapidly and shake its body from side to side as it walks in a single direction along the honeycomb' – to connect supporting information about the waggle dance back to the main idea.

As an extension, ask students to consider the thought-connectedness of this sentence from Darwin's landmark text *Origin Of Species*:

'Considering how flexible thin wax is, I do not see that there is any difficulty in the bees, whilst at work on the two sides of a strip of wax, perceiving that they have gnawed the wax away to the proper thinness, and then stopping their work.'

The main idea here is that bees have developed a building brain ('perceiving'). The connective participle clause 'considering how flexible wax is' supports his idea that there's no difficulty believing that bees can think it out. The supporting information about bees working two sides of a strip of wax is inserted as a subordinate clause. A conjunction – 'and then' – completes the main sentence action.

Now you try it
These connectives have been introduced earlier on in the book, but it may be helpful to students to be reminded of them:

- Sequencing: meanwhile, finally
- Contrasting: instead of, alternatively
- Comparing: equally, in the same way

Apply your skills
Further information is available on http://ag.arizona.edu/pubs/insects/ahb/inf10.html

Ask students to research all they can about bees and the environment before they begin writing. They should use their IT skills as well as referring to the library, newspapers and magazines.

Advise students that when writing persuasive essays, they can use the following paragraph bridges for specific purposes:

- to add information or continue a point – furthermore, in addition, to add
- to give examples – for example, for instance, to illustrate, my point is…
- to compare – similarly, likewise
- to contrast – however, on the other hand
- to conclude – in other words, in conclusion, to sum up

5 Shape ideas into cohesive paragraphs

Getting you thinking
Ask students to think about the following:

- A report has been written after a riot in a big city.
- A report has been written about a school's poor exam results.

In each case, who might write such a report?

Who would it be for? What would be its purpose?

Allow students to discuss the questions. There may not be right or wrong answers.

Now you try it
Allow students time to think about the proposal and then discuss their ideas in pairs.

Apply your skills

Students should use their IT skills, the library, newspapers and magazines to research ideas for the proposal and to set out their reports in a professional-looking way. This website may be particularly helpful to them: www.thesorrellfoundation.com.

End of unit fun

After completing the activities above, the class can play the paragraph game.

In small groups of about five, they need to decide on a story idea. They should work out who is writing the first paragraph, the supporting paragraphs and the final paragraph of this story (students can work individually or in pairs).

Each student writes their allotted paragraph, keeping to the agreed storyline.

At the end, they read out each paragraph in turn and see if they are cohesive. Could they be read as one continuous story?

The students should then work together to modify the paragraphs until they are happy with the story.

Chapter 5	Vary sentences for clarity, purpose and effect and write with technical accuracy of syntax and punctuation

1 Use punctuation creatively

Getting you thinking

Read the Thomas poem aloud several times or listen to a good recording.

The pauses after the full stops and the spaces between the stanzas help to create the summer silence at the little country station. The dashes express the process of memory. Someone has mentioned the odd name 'Adlestrop' and Thomas struggles to recall its associated memories. The commas and the lists that they help to construct allow him to recall what was close and then progress to what was further off on that summer day. This is truly creative punctuation at work.

Note also the enjambment in the third stanza, which contrasts with Thomas's use of full stops earlier in the poem.

How does it work?

Use the punctuation chart to find out which points are well understood by students and which are uncertain.

When writing description, it is helpful to use a colon to introduce and semicolons to divide. It is worth making a close study of the passage and its method.

2 Write expressive and varied sentences in descriptive writing

How does it work?

Remind abler students of the difference between defining and non-defining adjectival clauses.

A *defining clause* acts like a multi-word adjective. It is not marked off by commas.

For example: 'The brother who lives in Australia has become a champion athlete.' (There are several brothers but this particular Australian brother is picked out for praise.)

A *non-defining clause* just adds extra, non-vital information to the sentence. It is marked off with commas.

For example: 'My brother, who is marrying a girl from Yorkshire, won the TV Masterchef competition.' (The main point is winning the competition, and the Yorkshire girl is just an extra detail.)

Now you try it

Susan Hill's beautifully structured sentences of different lengths and patterns build up the tension and make the haunting very convincing. She uses a mixture of arresting short sentences and longer, complex sentences.

If necessary, remind students again of the definitions of simple, compound and complex sentences.

- A simple sentence consists of one clause. A clause contains a subject (someone or something) and a predicate (the other words in the sentence, which include a complete or finite verb).

The match started at two o'clock.

     S   V (predicate)

- A compound sentence contains two or more clauses of equal strength, each with its subject and verb, joined by conjunctions (joining words like and, but, or).

The players felt nervous but they played well.

   S   V   conjunction   V

- A subordinate clause contains its own complete verb. A subordinate phrase has no complete verb, although it may contain a participle, an incomplete verb form (going/gone).

- A complex sentence contains a main clause (the important idea) and one or more subordinate clauses or phrases (that depend on or explain further the main idea).

Both managers, who were worried about their jobs, watched anxiously as the players ran out onto the pitch.

(main clause/subordinate clause/main clause)

Apply your skills

A possible example could be:

Darkness was falling around me. I was alone, and yet I felt a presence in the half-light. Suddenly, I saw the black-clad woman with the wasted face. She stared at me, moving slowly in my direction.

Encourage the students to

- use fronted adverbials like 'slowly' and 'suddenly' at the start of their sentences

- use prepositional phrases at the start of their sentences ('In the half-light, I...')

- include phrases or clauses that act as adverbs, nouns or adjectives.

Encourage students to think about what could happen next. Here are some possible ideas:

- Arthur Kipps realises he is alone, except for the ghostly woman in black.

- He moves towards her but she vanishes.

- He looks around at the desolate scene.

- The calling seabirds seem to mock him.

Ask the students to think of four more ideas about what could happen before they start writing their extended pieces.

3 Shape sentences for effect

How does it work?

The writer has used sentence length and structure to capture the mood of the occasion.

The longer sentences at the start of the report build anticipation as the deadline approaches and crowds gather in Parliament Square. The two shorter sentences – 'We listened in silence.' and 'No statement was made.' – heighten the tension and draw our attention to what is said: nothing.

The writer uses a question to show the doubt and fear in the minds of the expectant crowd.

From this moment of silence, the final long sentence rushes outwards, with the dispersing people and their cry of 'War!'

Help students to understand how the longer sentences are constructed.

- Ask students to look at the final sentence. Can they find the two subjects and verbs of the main clauses? ('The great crowd rapidly dispersed...they cried out')

- What other verb forms can they find in the sentence? ('running', 'to get', 'as they ran')

- Show them how the subordinate phrases and clauses ('most of them running…', 'as they ran') are built onto the main clause.

- Finally, ask them what effect is produced by using a succession of verbs like this? How does it help to suggest the movement of the crowd?

Now you try it
Here is a good example of a dramatic scene described in six varied sentences:

A Road Accident

As the evening grew late, we flooded out of the cinema. The weather was dull and droplets of rain fell into the muddied puddles. Was that an old lady hobbling into the road? We watched her. Then came the awful event: a screech of breaks, a thump and somebody was hurt. I could hear voices shouting 'Accident!' 'Accident!' 'Accident!'

Apply your skills
You might want to look more closely at some of Aldington's sentences with the class to see how they work. Explain that the varied patterns make the meaning more subtle and expressive.

- Aldington opens with a clear and confident *compound sentence*: 'All the decay and dead of the battlefields entered his blood and seemed to poison him.' The rest of the paragraph then adds detail to this statement, and builds up to his final conclusion.

- Aldington adds extra description to a simple sentence stem with *subordinate clauses*:

  At dawn one morning when it was misty he walked over the top of Hill 91, where probably nobody had been by day since its capture.

- The sentence begins with an *adverbial phrase* started (or fronted) by the preposition 'At', and the meaning is developed through two adverbial clauses – 'when it was misty' and 'where nobody had been by day since its capture'.

- In the final sentence, the *main clause is delayed* and comes as a climax. Adlington builds up to his angry and sarcastic point – that this devastating war demonstrates the 'last achievements of civilised man' – with a series of subordinate phrases:

- 'Alone in the white curling mist, drifting slowly past like wraiths of the slain, with the far-off thunder of drum-fire beating the air, Winterbourne stood in frozen silence and contemplated the last achievements of civilised man.'

- He 'fronts' the sentence with three phrases – one based on an adjective 'Alone', one on a participle 'drifting', and one on a preposition 'with'.

Students can write their polemical paragraph as a letter, a newspaper column or a piece of powerful descriptive writing similar to Aldington's.

4 Write effective dialogue in stories and scripts

Getting you thinking
Possible answers could note that the hand is 'greyish white' and like a 'half-frozen toad'.

How does it work?
Ask students to list synonyms for 'says' and 'said'. They should stop at twenty. Then look in a thesaurus for others. Discuss the delicate shades of meaning that can be added to dialogue by these synonyms.

Now you try it
Here is a possible start for the dialogue:

'Oh, Jane,' whispered Ellen, 'I've seen that cold, white 'and again!'

'Oh, no,' cried Jane. 'I swear we've got to get out of 'ere or we're goners.'

'I'm so frightened,' moaned Ellen plaintively. 'The last time I saw that 'and it was beckoning me to come into the parlour!'

Apply your skills
Encourage students to think about what happens next. Perhaps Kipps describes the woman in more detail, while Jerome denies knowing anything about her?

Show students how scripts are set out. Refer to pages 38–39, where this is done.

- The character's name goes in the margin, followed by a colon.
- No speech marks are needed.
- Extra details of the character's behaviour or of the surrounding environment are put in brackets.

MR JEROME (staring nervously): A young woman? (There is silence in the lane).

Students could work in groups to try recording their scripts. Encourage them to share their recordings with the class.

5 Use rhetorical devices to make an impact

Getting you thinking
Students should pick out the patterns of these words as 'It was the…'.

They should work out that the pairs of words are:

- best/worst
- wisdom/foolishness
- Light/Darkness
- hope/despair.

Students should realise that the French Revolution offered hope and change but also stupidity, violence and death.

Now you try it
Students can work in pairs and read through the passage from *Animal Farm* several times.

They should pick up that Farmer Jones is seen as the big evil 'baddie', and that the last line is an appeal and a threat. The worst possibility (as the animals perceive it) is for Jones to take control of the farm again.

Apply your skills
Students should plan their ideas before they write their speech.

The class could – in groups or as a whole – choose a topic so that the speeches can be used in a group or class debate.

Allow students to give constructive feedback on others' performances. Whose rhetoric impressed? How could the speeches or their delivery have been improved?

6 Use formal grammar, including tenses and mood of verbs

Getting you thinking
The National Curriculum Guide wants pupils to recognise 'structures that are appropriate for formal speech and writing, including the subjunctive'. We may not pay a huge amount of attention to the subjunctive in English, but other languages do and students of French, German, Spanish and Italian will find the knowledge useful.

Students should avoid careless habits and use the subjunctive correctly. For instance:

'I wish you *was* my sister' sounds better as 'I wish you *were* my sister.'

Pip's convict in Dickens's *Great Expectations* says, as he hides out in the marshes after his escape from the convict ship, 'I wish I was a frog! Or a eel!' If he knew his subjunctive (and his indefinite articles), he would say 'I wish I *were* a frog! Or an eel!'

Now you try it
Tenses are straightforward but it is useful to know their various names. Irregular past tenses can cause problems. It is worth listing the most confusing of these in the students' grammar reference notes. *Gwynne's Grammar* (Ebury Press 2013) does this usefully (Appendix 2, pp. 156–162).

Apply your skills

The changes of tense in the Pliny passage are easy enough to make, but ask students about the effect of using the present tense on the drama of the passage.

More able students might like to add some further subjunctive-based sentences at the end of the passage, expressing the narrator's longing to survive and to escape the terror of the eruption.

1 Understand the effects of vocabulary choices

Now you try it

If the students have Internet access, www.etymonline.com is a very useful website.

During feedback on the formal written accounts, write some particularly good sentences on the board. Discuss the effects of the words chosen.

2 Develop a varied, ambitious vocabulary

How does it work?

Allow students to look up words that they are not familiar with. They could then experiment with the words by writing a short sentence for each word, placing it in context and checking that it makes sense.

Now you try it

Once students have found their ambitious words and written them into a creative paragraph (or two), they could then read their writing to a partner. The partner could suggest improvements to the paragraph, and students could redraft accordingly.

Apply your skills

Students could write a short play about somebody trapped in a rainforest, using as many interesting words as they can.

Extension

An extension task for more able students who finish early:

- Get into a group of three or four for a vocabulary game.

- One person has control of the dictionary (take it in turns). The person with the dictionary picks a complex or unusual word at random.

- The others in the group have to guess the meaning of the chosen word.

- Once the meaning is understood, the others in the group have to try to use it in an imaginative sentence. The person with the dictionary chooses whose sentence is the most entertaining and effective.

3 Use vocabulary with subtlety and originality

Getting you thinking

The first extract is from a novel by Fay Weldon; the second is from a short story by Jeanette Winterson.

How does it work?

Read the two texts aloud, then discuss them with the students. Try to draw out some of the following points:

- The first extract is reflective (considering what might have happened), giving the writing a slower pace. There is a mood of uncertainty ('or thought I was'), with lots of contrasting language to emphasise this (wonderful/terrible, sodden/dry). Specific nouns (oaks, maples) and the use of everyday objects (telephone, conservatory, garden) suggest realism and normality. The images are less imaginative than those in the second extract.

- The second extract is more dramatic, using verbs such as 'thrown', 'spilling' and 'explode'. The words are often unusual (linking shrapnel to flowers) and suggest a strange atmosphere of beauty (light, petals) and danger ('furious melt', burning). As well as the imaginative verbs, adjectives and adverbs, specific nouns (arum lilies instead of, simply, flowers) are used to add finer distinctions.

You could also discuss with students how the length of the sentences, in addition to the vocabulary used, helps to create atmosphere in each extract.

Now you try it
This task could be differentiated. Students sometimes find more dramatic writing easier to construct, so the less able could describe a house on fire.

Extension
Play a 'mood' vocabulary game in pairs. One person should think of a mood, such as excitement. The other needs to come up with five words or descriptions that would fit that mood (for example: high-speed chase; rollercoaster; shrieking with glee; heart beating, pulse racing; galvanise).

4 Choose vocabulary that is appropriate to your audience and purpose

Getting you thinking
The first extract is from a novella by Tom Baker called *The Boy Who Kicked Pigs*. The second extract is a piece of travel writing by Angela Carter, included in *Shaking a Leg* (collected journalism and other writings).

How does it work?
The first extract uses contrasting language and moods (die/marvellous) to create a shock and hook young readers. It also has a friendly tone ('makes you glad to be alive') and simple but effective descriptions ('to be young on a warm sunny Saturday').

The second extract paints a much more detailed picture for its older readers ('dusty cat rolls in the ruts') and features more specific details and ambitious images ('decent, drab kimono is enveloped in the whitest of enormous aprons'). There is a friendly tone ('somebody's aged granny') but more sophisticated references (Chopin). The class could also discuss the reasons for the different sentence lengths in each extract.

Now you try it
Students should work out that they need to change some vocabulary (such as 'nauseating') and phrases (such as 'soul-erosion').

Students might wish to alter the last two sentences to make the story more imaginative and entertaining for younger children.

Apply your skills
As an extension to the first task, students could also discuss how they would use design and layout differently, according to the target audience, to present their text.

The second task provides a good opportunity to challenge a more able group's perceptions of what appeals to boys and girls: as an extension, ask the class to read a few different stories by both boys and girls in the class.

Then ask the students whether there were any patterns in the types of story the boys chose and the types the girls chose. Is this what they expected? Get the students into mixed-gender groups of four, and ask them to discuss the kind of stories and vocabulary that they think appeals to boys and to girls. After this, feed back and discuss again as a class. Can we clearly define what boys and girls like to read? Have any students had their opinions changed?

1 Identify the building blocks of words

How does it work?
Students can work in pairs to recognise the different building blocks.

Now you try it
Students can also try this example:

- Agree –
- Agree – able
- Dis – agree – able

They can then find more words that they can make using 'agree'.

Apply your skills
As an additional exercise, students can see how many dis- words they can make.

Examples:

Dis – cipline

Dis – tribute

2 Improve your spelling of ambitious, complex words

Getting you thinking
To help them with the task, the class could be reminded of the spelling mantra: look – think – say – cover – write – check.

Apply your skills
The answers to the crossword are:

Across

extinguish, luxurious, joyous, contemplate, mercenary, xerophyte, yacht, innovative, phantom

Down

simultaneous, nausea, rheumatism, glisten, knowledge, turbulent, obfuscate, writhe, downgrade, artificial, burnished, urgent, venomous, hygienic, foreign, zeal, quaint

After the crossword exercise is complete, students can devise their own crossword.

Notes

Notes

Notes

Notes